REBOOT

IT'S TIME TO REBOOT YOURSELF

REBOOT

Your COVID-19 Quick-Start Guide
to Life, Work, and Hope

MK KIM

LIONCREST
PUBLISHING

REBOOT

Your COVID-19 Quick-Start Guide to Life, Work, and Hope

ISBN 978-1-5445-2137-4 *Hardcover*

978-1-5445-2136-7 *Paperback*

978-1-5445-2135-0 *Ebook*

To my employees and family, for their continued support and encouragement through the pandemic.

CONTENTS

4 Reboot Formulas

Reboot Formula 1: **On-Tact**
Connect through online platforms.

Reboot Formula 2: **Digital Transformation**
Debut your name in the digital world.

Reboot Formula 3: **Independent Worker**
Reboot yourself to become an independent worker.

Reboot Formula 4: **Safety**
Create all businesses with a safety sensitivity.

PROLOGUE

HOPING YOU'LL LEARN WHAT I'VE LEARNED

On January 22, 2020, less than a month after New Year's Day, I delivered my last speech of that year. I would have never guessed that it would be my last, but that's often how "lasts" work: they come without warning. Today you can remember the last day that you hopped on a subway without wearing a mask, the last time that you watched a movie in the theater with your sweetheart, or the day when you were excitedly pondering where to go for your summer getaway. But while it was happening, you didn't know that it was going to be the last time for a long time.

I've been a motivational speaker for most of my adult life, but coronavirus rocked that life to its very foundation. In all that time, I had never taken a break for more than a week.

Even in the midst of natural disasters, I still gave speeches. But in 2020, for the first time, the professional-speaking industry came to a halt so completely that there was no restart in sight. Since then, I have felt helplessly stranded in the unknown.

In the beginning, I thought it was a simple virus that would soon pass. Then, at the beginning of February, I thought, "Oh, wow. This is serious. It seems to be lasting longer than expected." I felt butterflies in my stomach. My morning routine used to begin with checking the day's speaking schedule, but my schedule, my car, and even I all came to a screeching halt.

"Boss, I'm afraid that we're going to be in serious trouble if this continues," said Director Choi toward the end of February. She was in charge of accounting at my company.

She said, "With the money reserved in our account, we might be able to hold out for a couple of months, but that's it."

My content-provider company was employing about twenty people. I also run a YouTube channel, MKTV, and an online college, MKYU(MK & You University), but the profits generated from these operations don't cover all of our expenses. The most established and reliable source of profit has always been my speeches. The pause in my speaking meant that the company was in jeopardy. I was full of anxiety as the days since my last speech stacked up. Then, one morning, I blurted out, "Please help me this one time to retain them all. Please grant my wish just once so that I don't have to let any of my employees go."

I had to do something, anything, to find a way out of this crisis and keep all my employees. Something had to change. So from that day on, I have had a new morning routine. I focused my nervous energy on problem solving. I began to fully prepare myself to find the answer to a question that I had never had to ask myself in my fifty-seven years of life: What do you do when faced with a highly contagious virus?

First, I subscribed to the print copies of two newspapers. I combed through every article, looking for answers in a world that was changing on a daily basis. I also subscribed to two weekly magazines. I read in-depth articles in order to get a firm grip on the issue. I requested regular mail subscriptions from domestic and foreign business-consulting firms to receive their reports. I also reached out to my younger brother, who is a college professor in the United States, and asked him for updated references from America.

Determined not to miss even the smallest clue, I read through books on economics, business management, trends, technology, humanities, history, and pandemics. The more information and knowledge that I accumulated, the more "human" clues stood out. My brain and body became busier than ever. I spent all my time trying to find clues, stopping only briefly when I had to sleep. My entire day was devoted to writing down ideas and thinking about solutions. If I had four clones of myself, it would still not have been enough. It was my desperate struggle to find "ways to survive in the post-coronavirus world."

About a month passed, and I started sensing that my search was going somewhere. My "coronavirus-solution notebook" was more than half filled. I found new clues each day, combined them with the ones I had found the previous day–disassembling and reassembling ideas with each piece of new information. Another month passed, and I started to see a glimmer of hope. I became convinced that the virus was not just a crisis but a door to another world.

And it all crystallized into this one mantra that kept reverberating in my mind: *order out of chaos.*

That was the answer. The more I learned, the truer it became. Despite closed businesses and deserted streets, life was beginning again. The entire world was teeming with newly emerging signs and phenomena. Once I had sorted out all the small, yet clear, signals, an order emerged everywhere I looked. I had to tell my employees.

At dinner, I said, "Life after coronavirus will be a completely different world. The formula for living and making money will be completely new. I've identified four formulas that will bring our company back to life. To make it happen, however, there is something we must do first. We must completely reset the way we operate our businesses. Let's reassess everything, removing anything unnecessary. We need to reboot!"

Over the next few months, our company charged ahead with rebooting all our business lines, clearing out anything that wouldn't fit into the changed world. It all went according to the four rebooting formulas. Five months into the crisis and, fortunately, my company has continued to function. My prayers were answered. Not only did I not let go of any of my employees, but I was also able to grow new business and hire new employees each month. It is all because I found a different way to connect to the world.

With those closest to me taken care of, I could focus my attention on others, outside our business. I had 1.1 million subscribers on YouTube and 15,000 students at MKYU, who were all affected by the coronavirus in one way or another. While working from home, a single mom was notified that her job was gone; a month after a restaurant owner opened up, he lost all his customers; and the owner of a small travel agency was drowning in a flood of canceled bookings and refund requests. Countless people were losing their jobs or businesses. Even worse, nobody knew the way out of the situation. All they could do was hope for the coronavirus to disappear and life to get back to what it used to be.

Looking at the distressed people around me, I decided that I should write a book. I needed to share with others what I had learned and do it properly. I wanted to find solutions not just for my own situation, but for all the people I cared about and wanted to comfort so they could save their work and life.

Several books had already been published that offered a macro view of the post-coronavirus world, but I wanted to write a book that addressed how the life and growth of individuals would unfold in this changed world. I wanted to address the question, "What does it mean to me personally? What should I do?"

In this book, I answer that question in five parts.

The key takeaway in Part 1 of this book is that hidden behind all chaos is order. If we see only chaos in the coronavirus-induced confusion and fail to see the order of the future, we will fail before we even start. The first key to overcoming this crisis is to find the order.

In Part 2, I present four Reboot Formulas that will change your life. The Reboot Formulas will help you identify the order necessary to move into the new world. The four formulas are what we use in my businesses whenever we plan for the future. They serve as the standards for evaluating risks and decisions. I'll outline each formula and offer ideas for applying them to your life or business in order to maximize your chances of thriving in the post-coronavirus world.

In Part 3, I will walk you through the process of writing a Reboot Scenario. If you're like me, you probably don't have the money or resources to commission a team of experts to come up with and evaluate all possible scenarios in the post-coronavirus world. Most of us have to come up with our own plan, based on what's most important to us. This practice will help you understand the specific obstacles that you face and plan for how you will address each in your own way.

Part 4 emphasizes the importance of becoming a "new learner" in order to keep your job in this period of digital transition. It is easy to degenerate into a "useless old-timer," whose college degree ensured a comfortable life. But in this fast-changing time, you need "just-in-time education" that you acquire quickly and apply immediately. In this section, I will share what I know about renewing yourself as an engaged learner.

Finally, in Part 5, I will address various questions that anyone who wants to succeed in this new world should ask themselves: "How can I survive in the post-pandemic world?" and "What is the underlying cause of the coronavirus pandemic?" I have concluded that this disastrous pandemic came about because of the indiscriminate exploitation of the environment our generation has been engaging in. In effect, we have been handing down heavier burdens on the future generation in order to satisfy our destructive greed. We must stand up and act if we want to prevent the next generation from living with a constant virus. I'm not an ecologist or environmental activist, but I have been deeply impressed by the people in these fields who have pointed out that we must make every possible effort to save the environment so that our children will have a better future. I will also try to answer the question, "How should we pull together to find courage and hope for ourselves as we stand amid this disaster?" I will talk about the "survival through relationships" that allows us to encourage, be considerate, and trust each other, and how to build a mental immunity that matters just as much as physical immunity at a time when the corona blues are consuming our hearts.

I wrote this book with a mindset completely different from the one that I had when I wrote my previous books. In those books, I primarily summarized what I had previously learned from personal experience. For this book, I wrote almost in real time, as I studied and gained insights into the ways in which I, myself, could survive. Never have I so desperately indulged in seeking answers and solutions for myself. Each time I found one, I cried out, "Eureka!"

It is my hope that readers will realize and experience everything that I have learned and experienced: the sense of relief that I felt when I found the order from this chaos, the thrill that I felt when I discovered the four formulas to beat this confusion, and the confidence that overtook me when I found the answer to surviving.

We've lost a lot in the wake of the coronavirus pandemic. We can no longer use public transportation without wearing a mask and children are not allowed to play as they wish. We make less money than before, and worse, many people have lost their jobs entirely, overnight. But just because we have lost so much doesn't mean that we cannot survive. We may have to put up with the loss of many things but not our survival. We must endure and survive no matter in what world we find ourselves.

Now is the time to end the "pause" and start to "reboot." Let's reboot ourselves instead of lying low–frustrated, worried, wounded, and defeated. Hope is still with us.

–MK Kim, June 2020

ABOUT THE TRANSLATOR: GUIHWA H. BLANZ

Guihwa H. Blanz majored in criminal justice at the C.W. Post Campus of Long Island University in New York. Prior to working as a translator, she worked as a journalist for the New York Korean language daily newspapers, *The Saegae Times* and *The Korea Central Daily.*

Ms. Blanz has translated over 200 Korean language books including the Korean record-breaking bestseller, *Youth, It's Painful*. She has also translated several English language books that became bestsellers in Korea including *The Nightly Book of Positive Quotations* and *Good Grief.*

PART 1

DON'T BE AFRAID OF A GRAND TRANSITION

The time to ask "When can I go back?" has passed.

Now is the time to take a deep breath and repeatedly ask, "How should I prepare for the coming future?" It's time to find clues for how to change little by little every day. We must train ourselves for a different way of life so we can enjoy the daily routines of eating, living, learning, and sharing. We must find solutions, on our own, with a sincere attitude toward life and a passionate attachment to it.

CHAPTER 1

CAN WE EVER GO BACK TO THE "BEFORE-CORONA" TIMES?

IT WAS NOT TEMPORARY; IT WAS THE BEGINNING

"When will this be over?"

In the beginning, each person I met skipped the usual greeting and asked this question instead.

"Who knows? I thought it'd calm down in a month or two, but here we are."

The responses were mostly the same. No one had a clear answer.

Next came the stage where everybody consoled each other.

"It's tough, isn't it? It's all because of this damn virus."

"Everyone's having a hard time these days. Just hang on. Hopefully, it'll be better soon."

At the time, we still had hope. I guess we could still afford to take it a little easy. But now, months later, I hardly find anybody having the same conversation. Everybody is experiencing panic in their own way, to varying degrees.

"This is going to ruin everything. Self-employed small businesses are closing, and larger companies are marching toward bankruptcy. You think it is about to get under control, but one new case appears, and everything is paralyzed again. I'm afraid this is going to last until next year."

We're feeling instinctively that some tremendous change is on its way. But we only get a glimpse of a dim silhouette, and the effects of coronavirus are so unpredictable that nobody can say definitively what will be next. Yet, there is a question that refuses to leave our minds: "Someday we'll go back to the days before corona, won't we?"

I met an old friend of mine a while ago—a veteran business-woman with extensive experience in corporate events. She has such an extraordinary passion and ability that she grew her company to fifty employees just two years after starting the business. Despite considerable authority and breadth of experience, her business collapsed irreparably when the coronavirus hit.

"Honestly, I thought everything would be fine if I endured for a month or two. But it continued to get worse. My business is about bringing a large audience to a location for an event. I've weathered natural disasters and freak situations, but nothing like this. Last week, a few employees came to me and told me that they were leaving because the company was having a difficult time. They asked me to bring them back when everything returned to normal...I was determined to hang on no matter what, but now I have lost all hope. I just choke up several times a day."

I also met a college buddy a few weeks ago. As a fifty-seven-year-old professor, he is only about eight years from retirement. He said that he's actually busier than before, trying to adjust to the online-class system now that colleges have stopped giving in-person classes.

"I predicted that the world would come to this point eventually, but I'm flustered because it came so abruptly. Professors are scrambling to deliver online classes. At first, I thought things would get back to normal, but this is unnerving. I'm afraid that I might have to continue online classes until the end of the year. I don't see any point in starting offline classes either, because once we have a single confirmed case in the class, we'll be right back to online classes anyway.

Everybody is in a panic right now—professors, the college, and students—because we don't know how to teach and learn or in what environment."

Everybody was intimidated by the coronavirus, even the talented, passionate businesswoman and the university professor with outstanding analytical skills. Everyone struggled to get through each day, and I was not an exception. I simply couldn't keep feeling this confusion.

With a sense of urgency, fearing that we might never go back to the old life again, I started studying. The balance of my bank account was quickly draining, making me toss and turn, sleepless until dawn. I was desperate beyond words. I was facing a matter of survival, for both my family and company. For several months, I've read thousands of pages of reports, met experts from all walks of life, and read page after page in newspapers, searching for clues to understand this new world. And then I arrived at a clear conclusion: This isn't coming to an end. The world as we knew it is over. We are already living in the new normal.

CORONAVIRUS WILL NEVER COME TO AN END

COVID-19 is marked by its powerful contagiousness. Unlike SARS or MERS, which had a low mortality rate, COVID-19 is so highly contagious that a single person can infect hundreds of people at a single large gathering. This infectious power caused our society to disintegrate instantly. Social distancing was the best response that we found to the mad spread of the coronavirus.

However, after a few months of social distancing, life didn't seem like a life anymore. I questioned whether this would ever stop. Even if we were to develop a vaccine, it was hard to believe that it would solve all our problems. As questions kept mounting in my mind, I met Choi Jae-cheon, a chair professor at Ewha Womans University. I thought that if anybody could give me clear answers on the nature of the coronavirus and what the future might be, he was the one.

When I asked him if we were ever going back to our previous routines, he told me, "The spread of coronavirus might slow down, but it will never come to a complete stop. People wish to hear that it has ended, but how can a virus end completely?"

"Do you mean that we have to keep living like this?" I asked.

"If humans continue to destroy the ecosystem to the point where we change the climate as we do now, a variety of other creatures besides bats will carry some type of deadly virus and strike us every two to three years. I mean, viruses will strike us at a speed faster than humans can develop vaccines for them."

"Then what do you suggest we should do?" I blurted the question out of desperation.

"I call social distancing a 'behavioral vaccine.' The only vaccine available for us at the moment is this behavioral vaccine. Going forward, we may have to learn how to coexist with viruses in the form of social distancing."

Prof. Choi's advice was sincere and born of having dedicated his entire life to the calling of being an ecologist. After leaving his office, one word lingered in my mind: coexistence. My illusion that the current situation is only "temporary" was also slowly disintegrating.

THE CORONAVIRUS-INDUCED MASSIVE TIPPING POINT

Malcolm Gladwell, author of *The Tipping Point*, equates the spread of the virus to the concept of a "social epidemic." According to him, all social epidemics have a tipping point: a moment where they break loose.[1] The concept of the tipping point can also be applied to marketing, and it is a marketer's job to proactively promote and sell a product or service until it becomes a trend, or reaches a tipping point, and makes many people purchase the product or the service. This time, however, all industries have reached a tipping point without having to spend money on marketing. In other words, coronavirus has played the role of a "global marketer" for them.

---

1   Malcolm Gladwell, *The Tipping Point: How Little Things Can Make a Big Difference* (Boston: Back Bay Books/Little, Brown, 2019), 7–14.

In April, *The Wall Street Journal* reported, "Adoption of robots and drones carrying goods speeds up as a frightened world craves safe delivery of everything from medical supplies to food."[2] The four-legged robot dog Spot approaches a patient and starts live broadcasting so that the patient can talk to a medical team remotely. A drone delivers the patient's vital signs to the medical staff. This is what's happening in the medical field while the coronavirus is rampaging.

The advances that the coronavirus accelerated affect every aspect of our society. Interpersonal relationships are shifting to online and robots are routine in medical services. Education takes place not in the classroom but on an online platform, and the workplace is moving from office to home. With every sector in our society having reached a tipping point of its own, we are standing on the cusp of an era of new standards, also known as the new normal.

The title of the 1972 paper "More Is Different," written by Nobel Prize winner Philip Anderson, points to exactly this phenomenon.[3] It is small changes, not a single big one, that accumulate to create a world that is qualitatively different. The world is becoming different as more individuals are

2   Christopher Mims, "The Scramble for Delivery Robots Is On and Startups Can Barely Keep Up," *The Wall Street Journal*, April 25, 2020, https://www.wsj.com/articles/the-scramble-for-delivery-robots-is-on-and-startups-can-barely-keep-up-11587787199.

3   P. W. Anderson, "More Is Different," *Science* 177, no. 4047 (1972): 393–96, https://doi.org/10.1126/science.177.4047.393.

intent on avoiding risks and crave safety. To be exact, it's not that the world is becoming different: it is us, individuals, who are creating a different world.

It's heartbreaking, but we must acknowledge the reality. Now is the time to take a deep breath and ask, "How should I prepare for the future?" We must find clues for how to change, little by little, every day. We must look for different ways in which to enjoy the daily routines of eating, living, learning, and sharing. We must find solutions on our own, with a sincere attitude toward life and a passionate attachment to it.

Of course, I still miss the world before coronavirus. I dearly miss the days when I got together with hundreds of people in a lecture hall, laughing and hugging each other, and patting the other's back. But now, I have come to realize a painful truth: I wish I could return, but I can't. I've already moved on to a different world.

CHAPTER 2

THE HIDDEN ORDER IN CHAOS

CORONAVIRUS IS NOT A CRISIS; IT IS CHAOS

"There is the world B.C.–Before Corona–and the world A.C.–After Corona."[4]

This is a quote from the column that Pulitzer Prize-winning columnist Thomas Friedman contributed to *The New York Times*. These terms for this period might actually appear in history books in the future. We've already crossed over to the world of A.C., and we have to deal with it no matter what the outcome may be. What on earth should we do? Where do we even start?

---

4   Thomas L. Friedman, "Our New Historical Divide: B.C. and A.C.–the World before Corona and the World After," *The New York Times*, March 17, 2020, http://www.nytimes.com/2020/03/17/opinion/coronavirus-trends.html.

It's scary and confusing, but there was a statement that came to my mind as I looked for a way to survive: crisis is an opportunity. It is something that was carved in the hearts of all Koreans when we went through the 1997 foreign-exchange crisis and the 2008 global financial crisis.

It is a statement that Koreans think of whenever we face a crisis—a statement that we have heard and said so much that we all have it memorized by heart. But words that you just "memorize by heart" are the most useless and vain ones. I've been a motivational speaker most of my adult life, but to be honest, the words in that statement don't come home to me. The word "crisis" somehow makes me feel emotionally intimidated, and the word "opportunity" sounds like something that has a lot to do with luck. More than anything, I cannot get the picture of how I can fit in—as the subject—between "crisis" and "opportunity."

Chaos is not just a meaningless fluctuation; it is a state where order can be created at any moment. In other words, it is a state that holds order within it.

According to *Order Out of Chaos* by Ilya Prigogine, winner of the Nobel Prize in 1977, many of the phenomena that we consider disorderly hold within them a considerably developed order.[5] Think about a swirling wave, for example.

_____

5   Ilya Prigogine, Isabelle Stengers, and Alvin Toffler, *Order Out of Chaos: Man's New Dialogue with Nature* (London: Verso, 2018).

To our eyes, the vortex may look chaotic, but the water's molecular structure tells a different story. The molecules may seem distanced from each other, but there is a certain order among them, and you can see a molecular structure that is arranged and structured in accordance with a certain rule. This realization completely changed what I had thought and imagined about chaos all those years. There it was, hiding in chaos: a neatly organized order that only looked chaotic and random to my eyes!

That got me thinking, "If that's how it works in nature, wouldn't it be the same with all the countless confusion and chaos that we experience in our lives? Wouldn't there be a new order forged within, as all those things are clashing and bumping into each other at the moment, even though we cannot see them at all? If I could draw the dynamic picture in advance and if I could only recognize it in advance, I myself might be able to become the main agent in the creation of the order of the world."

This realization remained forgotten for a while until the coronavirus brought it to light again. Heavily burdened with the responsibility of having to save the company, I wanted to interpret this crisis and find an answer. I pulled out the book that had been shelved all those years, dusted it off, and opened it. Reading the book again, I spent quite a long time racking my brain and thinking hard about chaos and order. Now the pandemic is no longer a nemesis that I feared or wanted to stay away from. I decided to accept this chaotic situation as another natural phenomenon.

HOW TO FIND OPPORTUNITY IN A NEW ORDER

If the energy of chaos is substantial, that means there is an even bigger order being forged within that chaos. In the wake of the coronavirus outbreak, our society seems to have come to a screeching halt, but if you look deeper, you can see that there is massive energy-creating movement. Chaos is forming where existing order and new order are clashing. Significant energy in chaos means that the scale of the order is likely to be much bigger in the end. So what we must do is find a way to become part of that order–fast!

My quest to find the order started with identifying "dots" in the chaos. The dots can be pieces of information, knowledge, or an awakening. If you start from one of these dots and connect it with another dot associated with it, then you have a line. Once you get this line, the previously meaningless dots become meaningful. And when you connect another dot to this line, you start to see a shape; soon, with enough dots, the shape grows into a real-life, three-dimensional object. The last stage in this quest, for me, was to find out where I stand in relation to that object and figure out an order that makes sense to me as an individual.

Entering an order means that an opportunity is fast

approaching because opportunities exist only within an order. The dots were ambiguous while I was searching for that invisible order. But before long, these little ambiguous dots that represented the knowledge and information that I had started growing bigger and clearer.

One example is the blockchain technology that I've been paying attention to since last year. Blockchain technology is called the public ledger, and it is "public" because all transaction data is shared and stored by all users who participate in digital networks, instead of being monopolized by conventional banks or only a few specific individuals. In the midst of the pandemic, I read a news article that reported that "people are avoiding using cash or credit cards because of the risk of contagion." I connected the dot that represented this change happening in the wake of the coronavirus outbreak with the dot that represented my knowledge of blockchain and realized that the widespread usage of digital currencies, controversial as they may have been, might start earlier than I'd thought.

Then I saw that the Korean government was providing universal basic income for disasters to its entire population. I saw people lining up at community centers to apply for the disaster relief, ignoring all social-distancing instructions. That led me to think that soon we might see the emergence of program money that can be exchanged and used by using the blockchain technology. Not long after, I read a news article about how Facebook is working on its own virtual currency, Libra. When I started with a dot representing blockchain and connected it to the dot representing the universal basic income for disasters and also to the dot representing Libra, the three-dimensional object that represented future currencies became clearer to me. The key point here is that these individually existing dots formed this dimensional object once I had the perspective to see them together.

The last step for me was to figure out how I could become a part of this "object": how I could apply blockchain to my business. I thought that if digital currencies are accepted for digital products such as a piece of content, it means that my speeches, books, or video content can also be bought and sold with digital coins. Suppose I upload videos on a platform and divide the shares in them into 100,000 coins at the price of ten cents per coin. When a video goes viral and generates profit, those who have invested in that video can get their returns in digital coins. In that case, I don't really need to use the YouTube platform to earn advertising revenue from Google.

The key to blockchain technology is that it removes the need for a middleman. In blockchain technology, every transaction and compensation are transparent. This is still in the idea stage, but I am trying to push myself into the dimensional object by making as many connections to my business operations as possible. When little dots are put together, they create order, and this order turns into an opportunity the minute that I engage in it.

The next dot that I focused on represented noncontact. It's a big dot and visible to everybody now that it has permeated every detail of our daily routines. I connected the noncontact dot to one formed by another news article I found. It said, "Coronavirus is behind the boom in the Netflix-type content business." This aligned with what futurist Dr. Choi Yoon-sik told me. He said, "The coronavirus is accelerating the development of artificial intelligence technology, and within just a few years, it will be developed enough to provide us with near-perfect foreign-language translation and interpretation. Language barriers between countries are disappearing."

When I connected the three dots that represented noncontact, content business, and artificial intelligence and put myself into them at the last step, an idea formed in my mind. The content business is growing, due in part to the fact that the coronavirus has forced people to spend more time at home. Those who craft good content products are recognized for their value. If the development of AI results in the breakdown of language barriers, I will have no obstacle to presenting my content products to overseas markets as well. The result is a much easier path toward breaking into foreign territories. If that happens, it will be possible to deliver my speeches to people in English-speaking countries and even around the world. The question then becomes, "How can I be prepared when that next opportunity presents itself?"

THE THIRD GAME-CHANGING OPPORTUNITY IS COMING

By now, most of us have accepted that a new future is coming. Unfortunately, we've been too consumed by the present, which is ever changing due to coronavirus, to realize that we're already there. Our collective future is jumping at an accelerated pace in the face of the massive storm in which we are living. The order that will slowly show itself after this chaotic storm passes is already taking shape.

A small number of people have noticed this new order already and are reacting accordingly. In Ho, a professor of computer engineering at Korea University who is the nation's top blockchain expert, says, "When there is a change from analog to digital, we call it a game change. When it happens, analog superpowers collapse in a flash, and new digital superpowers reign in the industry. The digital camera is a good example. When it was introduced, Kodak's stock became worthless paper. On the other hand, the emergence of the PC made Microsoft a global megacorporation, and the widespread usage of the internet made Google the top company in the world. Now the third game-changing opportunity is approaching. You cannot miss this opportunity."

The bigger the chaos, the greater the opportunity it brings. Those who are preparing now will see their wealth growing at a much greater rate than those who ignore the present chaos. At the same time, the polarization of wealth will get worse. Those who seize the opportunity will become richer, and those who miss it will become poorer. Once the storm of the fourth industrial revolution passes, along with the coronavirus pandemic, the gap between rich and poor is likely to grow wider than ever. The majority of individuals will be pushed out of the order, replaced by digital technology. Only a few of them will be able to jump on the bandwagon of wealth, as they have fewer opportunities and must compete over smaller amounts of capital. Just thinking about it makes me depressed.

The feeling is comparable to what I experienced during the 1997 foreign-exchange crisis. I was clueless about what was going on until I took a direct blow from the storm that hit the nation. I lost the apartment that I'd worked so hard to buy, and I had to move to the countryside and rent a room on a month-to-month basis; I couldn't even afford to get a long-term lease that required a deposit in advance. Just as the financial crisis was waning, I read an article that explained how the rich became richer while people like me were living from paycheck to paycheck. The crash had allowed them to snatch up three houses with the money that would normally have bought them just one. I cried for a long, long time after learning of the disparity. To me, the foreign-exchange crisis was a heartbreaking failure and nightmare.

But this time, there is an important difference. Now I am MK Kim, and I am fifty-seven years old. I am the head of a company, responsible for the livelihoods of more than twenty employees. With new perspectives and strategies, I was able to take advantage of the changing times. Right now, my company is running at an unprecedented pace. We're challenging ourselves and each other, hiring new employees, creating and investing in new businesses. We've transformed from a small content provider to a digital-media corporation. We've doubled our pace to keep up with the new opportunities.

Economic experts predict that the golden time to seize opportunities will last until a vaccine is developed and distributed. Once the chaos reaches its peak, the hidden order will slowly start surfacing. And the minute that everybody recognizes it and cries out, "So this is the new normal," the game will have already changed in the market. Those who foresaw, prepared, and invested in the new order will grab the upper hand in the market in a flash. There'll be no room left for latecomers. You and I must make it to the center of the chaos before the whistle blows to announce the expiration of this golden time. And there, we will have to create an order, if only a small one, that will ensure the sustainability of our jobs, our businesses, and our own selves.

You might feel as though you are standing in a thick fog. Things are fluctuating frantically, but if you look into the fog, you will see the dots hidden inside it. And if you can see them, you still have a chance. You can be the master of a new order if you connect those dots to your specific talents and goals. But if you cannot see an inch ahead of you, no matter how hard you look, you have only two choices: be pushed out of the order forever or start running forward. If you choose the former, please close this book without hesitation. However, if you choose the latter, no matter how difficult it is, I promise you this: you will figure out the order on your own and you will also create opportunities for yourself–as long as you take a brave first step into the storm of chaos.

CHAPTER 3

$$\boxed{}$$

I WON'T BECAUSE I CHOOSE NOT TO

Over the last few months, I've met so many people: intellectuals, CEOs, and leading authorities in their respective fields. I thought that considering who and what they were, they must already have answers. They must know where the world is headed. But the more I talked with them, the more it became clear to me that there are very few people who have answers!

I've met all kinds of experts, but it was rare to find somebody who could, based on reliable information and logic, give me a convincing analysis and explanation of what the post-coronavirus world would be like. It was same with their jobs and businesses. I thought that they must be connecting at least a few dots in order to manage their businesses and make predictions about their future. But I was wrong.

What is going on with these people, who are so smart and so full of passion? With all their accomplishments, why can't they answer the question that we've all been asking ourselves for months now? Then it dawned on me. The reason that the brightest minds still can't find the answers is that formulas are constantly changing. And the new formulas are extremely complicated. In the past, it was clear what people liked, what attracted people, generated profits, and would grow businesses. You could absolutely make a living by using the same formula that's been around for decades, touching it up with just a little innovation.

But the coronavirus killed the old formula and replaced it with a new one. New rules, such as noncontact and digital-first structures turned everyone's perspective upside down. The bigger the industry, the more likely people are to expect formulas to stay the same. But that is just a complacent delusion. It might work out that way if just one out of numerous industries were affected, but the coronavirus is affecting countless industries, including travel, restaurants, entertainment, and retail, not to mention big shopping malls and small businesses. It is pushing all those industries to the crossroads of life and death. We are in a situation where everybody is on their own to find a way to survive.

Those with more vested interests find it harder to squarely confront the situation. They cringe and step back because they are afraid to part with the sure thing–the proven money-making foundation, formula, and habit. The fear prevents them from exploring new formulas or even accepting that new formulas are necessary.

Perhaps it is human instinct to freeze in the face of the unexpected. But there is one thing we must remember every time that happens: while you are hesitating, the "second storm" is approaching.

Many of the changes that we believed to be temporary are going to be permanent. Children may not be able to return to school. Unpaid leave could end with massive layoffs. Companies might hang on for six months but not two years. The same goes for individuals. Soon, there will come a moment when companies and individuals will either go bankrupt or change their industries in order to survive. So now you have a serious question to ask yourself: "Did I really accept the post-coronavirus world into my life? Am I seriously determined to overcome this crisis by myself?"

THE GANGNAM-NEVER-FAILS LEGEND NO MORE

Choi Jae-bung, professor from the Department of Mechanical Engineering at Sungkyunkwan University and the author of *Phono Sapiens*, once told me about the kind of future-oriented talents that companies would be looking for.

A while ago, a fourth-grade elementary student participated in a drone competition and defeated grown-up competitors to win the grand prize. It turned out that he was from a small, rural elementary school that had only fourteen students in total, and he taught himself drone operation by watching YouTube videos. Do you know what he's learning right now from watching YouTube videos? It's coding and artificial intelligence. He is building a self-operating drone on his own. Don't you think I'd love to hire students like him if I were a CEO? In fact, the most successful IT companies these days don't care much about the educational background of job candidates. What they care about most is skills that can be put to use in the field right away because that's what they need urgently.

Experts knew that this formula would become universal in time, but the coronavirus accelerated its progress. That means that the prominent status that the eighth school district in Gangnam and the college-prep private academies in Daechi-dong have always held will tumble before long. Besides, if online classes become the new normal, what's the point of going to all those prestigious high schools in Gangnam? You don't really need to spend a lot of money to send your children to expensive private academies and live in expensive apartments in Gangnam. Naturally, this trend will depress the real estate market in Gangnam as well. It won't take long before the end of the "Gangnam-Never-Fails" legend.

In the longer term, we need to carefully observe the real

estate prices in densely populated apartment complexes in big cities because these urban apartment complexes are the most vulnerable to infectious diseases. If somebody is confirmed to have coronavirus, hundreds of people who live in the same apartment complex will panic. Experts are already predicting that a growing number of people will prefer houses and townhouses over apartments, and the demand for real estate in suburban areas and new cities will increase. Another factor contributing to relocation is the change happening in the way people work–at home rather than in an office.

Where to live and how to raise our children are important questions that will impact our future. In a transitional time like this, many people make decisions about the future based on formulas of the past. They follow formulas of the past because they are proven and the future is uncertain. But unless you apply new formulas, those of the past might not give you what you are looking for. The choice you make for your child's sake might become an obstacle to that child's future, and that important investment you make for the future of your family could result in a big loss.

Nobody is left untouched by the evolving formulas. Everyone, even those who aren't in charge of huge businesses, need to know how to understand the new context. We each need to be able to quickly understand new formulas and calculate the variables. You must make choices and design a new life based on the changes that you predict will happen at least one to two years from now.

There is no need to be frightened and intimidated even before you have a good idea of what is looming in the future. We have all already overcome countless difficulties while making a living. Each time we have hit a bump, we have kept moving on nevertheless, while learning, changing, sustaining, and even growing. It is a challenge worth taking up, even though it is nerve wracking and burdensome. Because, after all, all human affairs are created by humans.

DECLARE "I WON'T" INSTEAD OF "I CAN'T"

There are a significant number of readers who have already been hit hard by the coronavirus crisis. There is something that I really want to tell those who have been affected by the crisis and can no longer do what they used to: if you think that you can never go back to the pre-coronavirus days no matter how hard you try, stop telling yourself "I can't." Instead, declare "I won't."

About a month after the coronavirus pandemic was declared, I told my employees, "From now on, I am not speaking to audiences. Not because I can't, but because I won't."

For the first month after requests for my speeches stopped, the words I most frequently said to people were, "I can't make speeches because of the coronavirus." Every time somebody asked me how my speaking business was going, I repeatedly answered, "I can't." Then, at one point, I became irritated with myself. I thought saying "I can't" is what victims say. It means that I was a victim of the coronavirus; it robbed me. It is an answer that shows no commitment to finding a solution. I had been saying that for a month, and it was enough already.

So I changed my answer. I started saying, "I decided not to go and make speeches because, for one thing, the coronavirus has made it difficult to bring a group to one venue, and also because I don't want to create a potentially dangerous situation."

After declaring to the world that I wouldn't be making speeches anymore, my employees and I started searching for alternative ways to keep the company moving without my speaking engagements. With a new outlook, the answers started coming to us. And the same formula can be applied to your business and your life.

The first step to rebooting your life after the pandemic is to shift your perspective from "I can't" to "I won't." Just by changing our view of ourselves as powerless victims to empowered problem solvers, we find alternatives on our own. We cannot lose our firm grip on our lives under any circumstances. Let's not lose to the coronavirus. Let's declare with pride, "It's not that I can't; it's that I won't. And I bet you I'll resolve and overcome this crisis with my own power!"

PART 2

FOUR LIFE-CHANGING REBOOT FORMULAS

Now the turbulent times have passed, and we can breathe a little. Consumer spending that has remained frozen like ice is now breaking up and melting. Stores that have been closed are now opening their doors and getting ready to welcome customers again. Time that had paused for a while has started moving, and the post-coronavirus world is emerging.

Is your store, business, or service 100 percent ready for it?

CHAPTER 4

REBOOT FORMULA 1

ON-TACT

AN EMAIL FROM CALIFORNIA

For the first time in what seemed like forever, I received a request to give a speech for an audience. My excitement was through the roof. How long had it been since the last time I was asked to speak? Unfortunately, reality brought me back to earth almost immediately. Speaking in front of an audience was out of the question at a time when social distancing was mandatory. What's more, it didn't feel like the right thing to do. What if somebody was confirmed to have contracted coronavirus at my event? Just the thought of it was scary. I held back my excitement and told my staff in charge,

"Where could I even go right now? Where did the request come from?"

"It came from California, in America."

"America? How am I even supposed to get there? All airplanes are grounded, aren't they?"

"The client says that you can make your speech online through the app called Zoom. They will still pay you the same fee as for an in-person speech."

It turned out that a Los Angeles-based, Korean-owned company made the request because the owner of the company was a big fan of mine. Originally, he wanted to invite me to Los Angeles so that I could speak to his employees, but now that traveling was banned, his company was requesting that I give an online speech. They wanted me to cheer up the employees and boost their morale, which had taken a significant dip in the wake of the coronavirus outbreak.

I was shocked. I couldn't believe that they had requested an online speech. Not only that, they would pay my usual rate despite not getting the full, in-person experience. It was something that I could not ever have imagined in the past. The speaking industry typically only pays based on three elements: physical venue, audience, and speaker. There are all kinds of video lectures available today, but their prices are comparatively cheap because people have the impression that they are easily accessible for free on YouTube. Now I was being told that the value of my online speech was the same as an in-person one! Something that had seemed impossible before was now a reality, and it would not have been possible without the coronavirus. More importantly, that company's request wasn't a fluke: now I constantly receive requests from companies and local governments to make live online speeches.

Thanks to those first few online speeches, we started integrating new technologies into our daily lives. It wasn't long before Zoom, a previously unfamiliar app, was a necessity. One day, one of my employees suggested using Zoom for our welcoming ceremony and our Learning Lab event.

She was talking about MKYU, of which I am president, and the Learning Lab event, which is a small-scale, off-line speaking event for honor students. The ceremony to welcome new students to MKYU and the Learning Lab events had been scheduled for March 2020. For obvious reasons, they were both canceled. Instead of leaving the students with nothing, now that we had had some practice, my team suggested moving those events online.

In no time, Learning Lab moved online for the first time in MKYU's history. About thirty students were invited, and to my surprise, the response was incredibly good. I had been worried about it, believing that many students were not familiar with online events, but it was an unnecessary concern. The students who participated in the Learning Lab from their home joined the conversation comfortably, and they quickly became familiar with each other over the internet, while introducing themselves and asking questions. Sometimes their family members inadvertently made short appearances in the background, and these added more fun to the whole session. The atmosphere of the event was particularly unique to the off-line alternatives because overseas students could mix with students from local cities, something that would have been impossible if they were all required to travel to Seoul for the event.

Encouraged by the successful Learning Lab event, MKYU went on to successfully hold the freshmen welcoming ceremony online in May 2020, by utilizing YouTube Live. About 500 new students pledged the admission oath in real time, participated in orientation, and asked diverse questions about college life. Even though it was an online event, their feedback was very positive. Many of them expressed how they felt their hearts warming when pledging the admission oath and how they felt choked up when they realized that they were going back to college. It was an online ceremony that created just as much anticipation and excitement as an offline one would have. MKYU decided to offer all classes and meetings online from now on. This shows how we started finding measures, small as they may be, to fill the gap between contact and noncontact gatherings.

At the same time, I am also scheduling more virtual paid speeches to reach more people and generate revenue again. That is the best way that I have I found to make the one-and-a-half-hour, on-stage speeches that I had always wanted to, instead of offering fifteen-minute-long YouTube videos. It would have been a difficult challenge to take up if the value and impact of noncontact events hadn't become as similar in-person events as they are now.

CONNECT WITH THE WORLD THE WAY BTS HAS

I am now a woman in my late fifties. It was not too long ago that I had little interest in the digital world, but the changes brought by the coronavirus forced me to pay attention to it. My digital skills were just enough to feel comfortable using word-processing programs and uploading them to social media. In fact, it would be more accurate to say that I used those apps and programs without really knowing that they were part of digital technology.

I thought, "What would have happened to me had there not been digital technology? What a great relief." If there were no platforms such as Zoom or YouTube, I wouldn't have been able to speak online, let alone off-line. I also wouldn't have been able to protect my employees' or my own livelihood.

We cannot live the way we used to. In the "no-contact" era, the only way to connect us is online. The internet continuously connects us to the world as we work, meet people, and buy daily necessities. We have moved on to what some people call the "on-tact" (short for "online contact") era, where we are all connected through online platforms.

The concept of "on-tact," which describes how people can build and enjoy deeper connections online, quickly changed everything that we had thought to be impossible into possible. There is no better example of how far an on-tact mindset can take us than the most famous K-pop group, BTS. To make the most of a horrible situation in which all concerts were canceled, BTS decided to stream a live performance for all audiences who wanted to attend. There would be no live, in-person audience, but the concert did allow for fans from all over the world to stream the show. "Bang Bang Con: The Live" recorded over 50 million views and 2 million concurrent viewers in a span of twenty-four hours.[6]

Fans individually logged on to BTS's community platform, Weverse, from their rooms, connected their light sticks–called "army bombs"–to Bluetooth to display different-colored lights as they cheered for the band. It looked as though all the fans from around the world were

---

6   So-yeon Yoon, "BTS's 'Bang Bang Con' Gets More than 50 Million Views over the Weekend," *Korea JoongAng Daily*, April 20, 2020, https://koreajoongangdaily.joins.com/news/article/article.aspx?aid=3076266.

gathered together in one place, cheering as one for the artists. It was reported that about 500,000 army bombs, from 162 regions around the world, were linked together during the concert.[7] It was a marvelous event that simultaneously connected millions of fans across borders by using on-tact technology. Rave reviews began pouring in immediately after the concert, some suggesting that BTS had created a new way of performing in the noncontact era.

Art exhibitions used to be something that you enjoyed in person, but now museums and galleries are adopting on-tact technology to shift to online exhibitions. The Savina Museum developed a program to make exhibitions available through virtual reality (VR), and to date, the museum has produced a total of twenty-nine VR exhibitions. As of March 2020, the number of VR views increased tenfold from the previous month.

The department store industry took a direct hit by the coronavirus, but the industry is also joining in this change. In April 2020, Hyundai Department Store hosted the first "digital live fashion show" sans audience and broadcast live on the internet. The show was staged to have designers of the brands that were showcased in the fashion show make an appearance and explain their products and fashion trends—all online.

---

7   Ibid.

Food companies have changed their off-line cooking classes to online ones, and construction companies are presenting cyber model houses. Banks have also urgently created a system in which customers can receive asset management counseling via smartphone video calls. The world is adapting to on-tact faster than we thought it would.

The digital technology that has been improving for over twenty years is what makes on-tact possible. Korea was the first country in the world to commercialize 5G technology, which is the core infrastructure of the fourth industrial revolution. Amazing things happen when digital is paired with 5G, which makes ultra-fast, ultra-connectivity possible. Anyone can predict the tremendous progress that will happen in remote education and telemedicine fields, as 5G reaches all corners of the globe. Digital technologies are evolving in a variety of ways, at tremendous speed, to fill the massive gap created by social distancing. In order to survive in the age of on-tact—which is the changed formula of the world—you must look for ways to narrow the gaps and distances with on-tact technologies and start applying those technologies, beginning with the easier ones, to your job and business.

WHAT DOES IT TAKE TO BE READY FOR ON-TACT?

Gyuri has been a consultant on MKTV for more than a year, and she is also an English tutor. For years, she's been teaching students, both privately and in groups, and she specializes in tutoring for the English portion of the College Scholastic Ability Test (CSAT). When I bumped into her after several months of being stuck inside, I asked her about her job situation, which concerned me.

"How's your teaching job going these days? You must have almost no classes."

"Not really. I'm working hard teaching kids these days. It's all thanks to you."

"Huh? Thanks to me?"

"Well, I'd been hesitating about whether or not I should start a YouTube channel. I monitored your videos and, as a consultant to MKTV, suggested content ideas. I felt inspired. So I started a YouTube channel last year. As soon as the coronavirus broke out, I immediately started teaching classes through YouTube Live. The response from the kids is better than before, now that I have incorporated a blackboard to write notes on top of streaming the lessons. They focus better, too. My classes haven't been affected at all. None of my students canceled their subscription."

According to Gyuri, the feedback from both students and parents has been good because small class settings allow both teacher and students to better prepare:

This situation has been a big awakening for me because I realized how individuals and freelancers like myself can survive even the coronavirus crisis, if they have the right skills and are capable of using digital technology. Thank God, I was prepared for all this in advance. If I had tried to start after the coronavirus crisis began, I might have felt overwhelmed at the thought of having to learn everything all at once. I think I would have given up in the middle of it all, and it would have been difficult to keep my job.

Gyuri is in her mid-fifties, close to my age. Nevertheless, she is always interacting with passionate young people, and because of that, she was exposed to new technologies. Gyuri was ready for the on-tact era before she even realized it.

The spirit of on-tact is about taking the initiative to move forward to connect with the world. On-tact is the future that is already with us, no matter what industry or business you are in. It is something that everybody is sure to encounter someday. It is important to be prepared for it and to approach it proactively. To make that happen, you have to take that first step. Remember, those who move ahead of trends do not take their first step because they have accurate knowledge of the future. They just take their first step blindly, believing in the small dots that they could connect and understand.

Gyuri did the same. She felt nervous when she remained

stagnant. To overcome her nervousness, she proactively learned whatever she could. Even while studying, she must have wondered if it would make any difference. She must have been tempted to give up the YouTube channel many times, when she saw that the number of subscribers did not increase much, even though she bought YouTube equipment and uploaded videos that she'd worked hard to make. Nevertheless, Gyuri did not give up, and eventually, she realized her own on-tact.

Among the freelancers whose livelihood is directly dependent on going online, there are quite a few who are making timely moves. They know that they are on their own to figure out exactly how the money moves and to grab opportunities when they present themselves. On the other hand, those who are employed by a company may not be so keyed into the on-tact trend unless they are working in relevant departments. They don't even bother to think about how to reconnect the broken channel between them and their customers. But now, even their jobs are not secure. Technology and connectivity are being updated rapidly, so no one can be sure of how long they will remain in a company, department, or position. They will soon feel the sense of urgency with which freelancers are all too familiar.

Even under the dark clouds of coronavirus, there are essential elements in our daily lives that never change: what we eat, how we sleep, shop, meet people, and work. The only way to unclog the channels that are blocked by the corona-virus is to immediately start taking whatever actions you can to incorporate on-tact into all these areas of your life.

Even if you're not sure that the project you want to start will be successful, you have to go ahead, even if you are uncertain. At a time when the world is full of uncertainties, winning and losing depend on who starts first and how fast. A small but fast first step, taken courageously, will transform you into somebody who is fit for the on-tact era. On-tact can be your answer, but only if you connect yourself imme-diately. The shortest way to realize the first formula, on-tact, depends solely on your willingness to connect.

CHAPTER 5

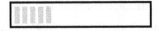

REBOOT FORMULA 2

DIGITAL TRANSFORMATION

"It would be awesome if you were my big sister. Then you could nag me and coach me in ways to have a better life, while living under the same roof with me."

"I know. That would be great, but I only have one body."

This is a conversation that I frequently have with people who attend my speeches or watch my videos. I can read sincerity and earnestness in their eyes when we talk. I have many fans who are younger than me and would like me to be their mentor. It is not possible because I'm always so busy that I hardly have time to see my own children and employees as often as I want to. But what if it could really happen?

Not long ago, I read an article about an English-speaking artificial intelligence robot. According to the article, a company called AKAAI supplied an artificial intelligence robot, Musio, to be a learning assistant at Mureung Elementary and Junior High School, an innovative school on Jeju Island. Musio can communicate fluently in English, thanks to the deep-learning algorithms that power it. The robot can read children's feelings and make faces as well. The whole thing was remarkable. When I read this, I started to imagine the possibilities.

In my imagination, I thought of the day when I could tell my employees, "You know something? I think I can be a robot, too. I need big data and AI to make it happen. That's important, and I think I know how to do it. First, I would collect data, including personal information about my fans, such as their age and occupation, and I would also collect data on their consumption habits, hobbies, interests, and favorite book genres. Then I would analyze the big data by using AI and deep learning and practice how to ask and answer questions." Think about the movie *Her*. It's entirely possible that I could become *Her*.

I would then have to go through the same process for myself. I would collect all messages and solutions that I have given up until now before using AI and deep learning to build an MK Kim Coaching Program, using that big data. Suppose someone asked me, "MK, what book do you recommend that I read today?" I would then ask the person a few questions and recommend a book that would be just right for them. I could make a wake-up call to my users, nag them to get up and ready for school, and I could also comfort them when they were sad and admonish them when they were lazy. It would be like supplying the adults in every household with an MK Coach. It would be a robot coach that gave people personalized answers to all their questions.

Even in my imagination, I predicted that my employees might all have a similar look on their faces—one that said, "What's got into our boss's head to make her go on about a robot like that?" But they would be supportive, as they always are.

One of my employees might ask, "Does that mean that you enter a monitor like in the movie?"

"Well, I should go for something fancier than that, don't you think? You know, there is a technology called the Internet of Things. What if I introduced a speaker that has this technology built into it and called it AI MK Kim Coach. Users could signal me 'MK' and ask me questions, which I would answer in my own voice, the way Alexa does. If the app works on smartphones, people could use it while on the move. With 4D printing technology on the way, users could see an angry MK, a smiling MK, a staring MK, and many other MKs in 4D printing and keep them on their desks. If augmented reality were added to the device, I could even appear in the air, like Genie in the storybook *Aladdin*."

"Oh, wow. Is all that really possible?"

"Of course, it is possible! Not everyone knows it, but such technologies are almost in the last stage of development. With each advancement, the technologies also become more affordable and precise. They are already available for practical use–think about robotic vacuum cleaners."

In truth, many of the technologies listed above are already available and commercialized. But the exciting part is that we're just getting started. Even more amazing advancement is possible. There are roughly 100 core technologies that were developed during the fourth industrial revolution, and at this very moment, these technologies have been brought together to create new synergistic technologies. For example, 3D printing technology is moving beyond simply printing out the objects that are entered; it is evolving into 4D printing technology, which changes the shapes of entered objects depending on various environmental factors, such as heat, vibration, and air.

Technology aside, what makes a robot able to engage with and coach the user appropriately? The secret lies in artificial intelligence algorithms. Algorithms can learn more about people and our behaviors than we know ourselves. Algorithms that are developed by studying data from millions of people are already smarter than humans. Hyperpersonalization technologies make it possible to create individuals' profiles based on big data–for example, Netflix, which knows which movies you would like to watch before you do; Instagram ads that know better than you which products you need; and Amazon, which identifies your daily necessities and delivers them to your door when you run out of them. It is algorithms that, by analyzing data, make it possible for these companies to have personalized communication with individual customers and deliver the products and services that they need. Therefore, AI MK Kim Coach is not just an unrealistic dream.

The state in which I can overcome the limitations of being the single human MK Kim and connect unlimitedly with many devices and people through digital technology is what I call hyperconnectivity. Hyperconnectivity refers to the possibility of moving beyond time and space to achieve the unlimited expansion of the range of connections: person-to-person, person-to-machine, and machine-to-machine communication.[8] Super intelligence is what makes this hyperconnectivity possible. Super intelligence refers to artificial intelligence that far exceeds human intelligence. Super intelligence is the technology that gives computer programs

---

8   "Hyperconnectivity," Wikipedia, last modified January 13, 2021, https://en.wikipedia.org/w/index.php?title=Hyperconnectivity&oldid=1000089145.

the ability to learn, reason, and self-develop—all functions of which until now only humans were considered capable.[9]

In short, hyperconnectivity is about connecting, without physical restrictions, by using intelligence that is superior to that of humans. Hyperconnectivity is emerging as a powerful alternative to resuming our daily routines, which came to a sudden halt due to the coronavirus. Hyperconnectivity is the choice that we make in order to deal with the current situation in which life has been put on pause and which is the culmination of the fourth industrial revolution.

I'm neither an engineer who is developing digital technology nor somebody who has studied it professionally. However, I came to learn about hyperconnectivity while frantically exploring the changes happening in the world in the wake of the coronavirus pandemic. Thankfully, my exploration gave me a glimpse of the latest technologies that have been developed and made available to us and of how those technologies are being used to manufacture various products. These advances were no more apparent to me than while I was looking at a smart refrigerator and imagining the not-so-distant future.

I thought about how the refrigerator is built on big data, artificial intelligence, and Internet of Things technology. In a

---

9   "Superintelligence," Wikipedia, February 16, 2021, https://en.wikipedia.org/w/index.
     php?title=Superintelligence&oldid=1000476760.

year or so, hyperpersonalization technology might be added to it so that a seriously upgraded refrigerator might become available. If it is connected to online grocery-delivery services, such as Market Kurly and SSG, would recommend meals for me, and it would also order food ingredients and have them delivered to my door. All I need is a cooking robot, and I will be completely free from kitchen work. I can't believe that a brand-new world is coming so soon, and I can't wait to see it!

This was how much I was able to imagine, given how much I understood. A little sketchy, perhaps, but this way of thinking is extremely helpful in understanding the latest digitized world.

WE ARE ALL BIG-DATA PRODUCERS

Big data and artificial intelligence are increasingly becoming an integral part of our work and business. I am often surprised when I log into my YouTube channel and click on the YouTube Studio where I manage it. Not long ago, when I uploaded videos, I could only see numbers, such as the number of views, the number of subscribers, and the amount of money I made from them. It was entirely up to me to analyze what these numbers meant and what to do to promote my channel in the future. But these days, YouTube analyzes my data and explains it to me.

Not only does YouTube show me the rankings of all my videos, but it also congratulates me by dropping confetti when any of my videos are ranked number one. It nags at me if any of the videos have received few views, telling me that only a small number of my subscribers clicked on that video and, even when they did, they didn't stay long to watch it. If profits continue to drop, it suggests that I need to increase the number of ads in the video and make it more advertiser friendly. It seems only a matter of time before the YouTube version of Alexa or Siri makes a debut.

I turn to YouTube algorithms when I look for materials for new YouTube videos or when I make thumbnails and add hashtags. I search for keywords that women in their thirties and fifties are most likely to be drawn to. If I can include those words, I can attract more viewers and subscribers to my channel.

Since our company established a self-development-themed e-commerce website called So It Begins, I often turn to Google to ask questions such as, "What are the school supplies that people need most when they study?" or "What are the most frequently searched products related to working from home?"

This is how we have easy and convenient access to big data, while advanced algorithms are making search engines such as Google and Naver more powerful than ever before. Where there is big data, there are algorithms, and algorithms are trusted by the majority of people. People become more and more dependent on algorithms because algorithms can give them just the answers that they need, and their power grows stronger as the number of users increases.

Last year, I interviewed Cho Sung-joon, a professor of industrial engineering at Seoul National University and the author of *Big Data: A New Language to Read the World*, on my YouTube channel. At that time, the professor told me, "In the digital age, big data is like wheat grains. No matter how good artificial intelligence is, you can't make it into something useful, like bread, without big data. In reality, we are all big-data producers. In other words, we are digital farmers."

I couldn't agree with him more. I was generating big data each time that I entered a word into the Google or You-Tube search bar and each time that I made a purchase. So why was Google, instead of me, making all the money? It wasn't fair. It was only using it because of the convenience, and I had never thought about how it was building massive wealth, thanks to me. For the first time, I thought that I should take back ownership because I was also one of the big-data producers.

Then I happened to meet Oh Jong-chul, CEO of Parastar. Mr. Oh has been running a motivational speaking agency, developing and hosting motivational speech events for companies, while also making speeches himself. Then a few years ago, he founded a startup company and launched a website called Parastar, which connected Instagram influencers with companies that wished to promote their products on Instagram. When I met with him, I took the opportunity to ask him to look at my Instagram account. He pulled out his iPad and entered information about my account. About five minutes later, stats on my account that I'd never seen before started popping up on his iPad.

The stats included the ranking of my account and a list of keywords that summarized the message of my account and the impression that it was giving to visitors. The keywords came from the analysis of the characteristics of my account and the traits of my followers, and they provided me with perfectly accurate data that I could use to develop Instagram-based business strategies. The interesting part was that the stats made it possible for me to predict the number of potential purchasers who might like the products that I promoted on my account. Of course, I would not attempt to become an influencer dedicated to selling products on my account, but the analysis and prediction were amazing to me.

"This platform uses AI to give customers the analysis of their accounts by using the big data of Instagram. When we analyze our customers' accounts, it provides such accurate statistics that we are getting great feedback from our customers. They can build business strategies while checking their stats in real time, which means they dramatically reduce the risk of failure."

Parastar is a startup founded by three like-minded people, and now it has grown into a company with more than ten employees. It is growing fast by applying digital technology to its business. CEO Oh told me that such service is possible only as long as there are competent designers and developers. These days, many platforms just like Parastar are being launched for Instagram influencers. This indicates services that analyze big data are becoming the industry standard.

Many of today's websites and online shopping malls show that these technologies have already became part of our daily lives. Even small-scale online shopping malls are using chatbot technology in which robots deal with customer inquiries and recommend products that customers might like.

Digital technologies are not exclusive to large corporations. We should no longer remain passive providers of information for large corporations or users of just a small part of what big data provides. We should try to become the producers and suppliers who proactively apply these technologies in our work and businesses. No matter how intimidating those technologies may be, anybody can benefit from them, as long as they know how to dissect and divide them for practical use.

IS THE LUXURY BRAND BURBERRY A DIGITAL COMPANY?

Now that digital technologies are within our reach, what is the next important thing? You must integrate your business, yourself, your brain structure, and digital technology. Apply the "transformation"—a much-talked-about subject among companies—to yourself as an individual. Transformation is more than just change. It is a thorough, dramatic, fundamental shift. Think about the metamorphosis you see in the movie *Transformers*, where the main character, Bumblebee, changes itself from an old, ordinary car into the strongest combat robot in the universe. When I say digital transformation, I'm referring to a business management strategy that creates all-new systems for corporate strategy, organization, process, and communication by going digital. Take, for example, Burberry.

Burberry is a luxury brand that many people are familiar with. If I ask people what kind of company it is, they are likely to call it some version of a luxury fashion brand. But Burberry defines itself as a digital-media company. If you're confused, you aren't alone.

At the time of the 2008 global financial crisis, the image of the Burberry brand, as well as company sales, were taking a deep dive. To save it from complete ruin, Angela Ahrendts, the then-CEO of Burberry, declared that the company intended to shift its business model to "become the first fully digital luxury company."[10] The company would push forward with this "fully digital" strategy, going digital in every aspect of the business.

Since then, Burberry has replaced core human resources with digital-savvy talents who "lived and breathed digital." In 2014, it was estimated that 70 percent of employees at Burberry's UK headquarters were under thirty. Concerned that young employees might be overwhelmed by the authority of Burberry, with its long history and tradition, and would not speak up to offer their opinions, the company took various measures to foster effective communication, both internally and externally. In a move that may shock many people, management even encouraged employees to actively use social media at work![11]

With this new digital culture in place, Burberry pushed forward with online campaigns and fashion shows by leveraging various social networks. In 2009, it became one of the first luxury brands to launch its own Facebook page,[12] which went on to amass 1 million fans before the year's end.[13] Then, in September 2011, Burberry used YouTube, Twitter, and

---

10 Robin Swire, "Why Is Burberry's Digital Strategy So Good?" Parallax, April 28, 2014, https://parall.ax/blog/view/3047/why-is-burberry-s-digital-strategy-so-good.

11 Ibid.

12 Ibid.

13 Yousef Khan, "How Burberry Embraced Digital and Transformed into a Leading Luxury Brand," Centric Digital, November 9, 2015, https://centricdigital.com/blog/digital-strategy/digital-transformation-in-traditional-fashion-burberry/.

Instagram to unveil its coming year's collection before the actual launch event.[14]

When Burberry launched Burberry Bespoke, an online service personalized for individual customers, they were able to craft designs that they knew customers wanted. Their customers were able to choose everything to their personal taste: silhouette, fabric, color, design, cut, size, and so forth. Choosing among these various elements gave customers 12 million options![15] Burberry proved itself to be the king of personally customized service, providing customers with a luxury brand designer and a tailor who could provide them with just the right wardrobe, made just for them.

Now that the company has used digital technologies to change everything, including the organization, strategy, production, and marketing, nobody can refute that Burberry is a digital-media company, as originally declared by CEO Angela Ahrendts. Thanks to this digital transformation, between 2008 and 2012,[16] Burberry doubled its revenues and operating income, and between 2002 and 2018,[17] its share price jumped by as much as 660 percent. This is how

---

14   Ibid.

15   Angela Ahrendts, "Burberry's CEO on Turning an Aging British Icon into a Global Luxury Brand," *Harvard Business Review*, January–February 2013, https://hbr.org/2013/01/burberrys-ceo-on-turning-an-aging-british-icon-into-a-global-luxury-brand.

16   Ibid.

17   Osman Husain, "How Burberry Saved Its Brand by Focusing on Digital," eMAG, February 25, 2018, https://emag.live/how-burberry-saved-its-brand-by-focusing-on-digital/.

the "Classic Burberry" that we have been wearing since our mothers' generation made a full transformation into "Digital Burberry" by integrating itself with digital technologies.

BECOMING A DIGITAL TRANSFORMER

Many companies besides Burberry have accomplished digital transformation. While studying various corporations, I asked myself, "Is my company a digital company?" People might think it is, considering how my company is running a YouTube channel that boasts 1.1 million subscribers and has also established an online educational platform, MKYU. But as the president of the company, I know that nine out of ten systems in my company still remain antiquated analog. We use digital technology and online platforms, but they are restricted to a few areas, and most others–HR, organization, communication, products, and marketing–remain analog.

Because I am the leader of the company, in order to accomplish a true digital transformation, I need to first revamp my own way of thinking. It was in this spirit of transformation that I told my team, "Our company should be a 'digital company' whose core competitiveness is content. We cannot deliver our content to customers and have them experience what we offer by following the old way anymore. Imagine if we went digital in every area of our company. What do you think it would be like? We can survive only if we transform our company into a digital company."

In fact, at the moment I am preparing to recruit IT professionals to work for my company. The team will be set up by this summer. I am also planning to change communication tools and adopt the latest marketing tools. The most urgent priority for now, however, is to integrate digital into my brain, and the biggest challenge is how to digitize the current online education site. Several times a day, I keep building and destroying something new in my head. I imagine how my company will be transformed by bringing in artificial intelligence to the company one day, Internet of Things the next day, and sometimes by bringing in everything that I can think of, all at the same time. During this process, I went so far as to come up with the previously mentioned idea of AI MK Kim Coach. Now that I have imagined myself transforming from analog motivational speaker MK Kim to an AI MK Kim robot, I can say that I have accomplished my own transformation, albeit only in my head.

I'm only at the practice stage at the moment, but there is something that is clearly different from the past: my view on data. My company frequently hosts small and large events for customers, and each time that there is an event, I ask my staff about the event's landing page. I ask them what outcome we want the event to have. In the past, I used Google forms because of their convenience. Unfortunately, that meant that all data remained on Google. My company did not retain any useful data. But if I can get my customers to join my website or become my followers on social media, information about them will become my own big data. Data is the most expensive and valuable tool in the digital world. If I have data, I can further segment the needs of my students, subscribers, and customers and provide them in a personalized way.

In the past, in order to understand which services to provide to students, I had to hold two-or-more-hour meetings with student representatives and my employees. Since bringing in many people for a meeting was not so easy, I could have those meetings only when I needed to make important decisions. Therefore, all I could do most days was read the comments and reviews that students made on my social media channels, including my blog. I was completely analog.

But once I started using the big data of my customers, a completely new world opened up for me. If I collect and organize it well, big data can be a virtual "entity" with which I can ultimately "have a conversation" about my business. I can ask big data what my customers truly want, and I can provide services that are personalized for individual customers. It is something I had never thought of when I was living in an analog world. But now that I have changed my mindset and perceive myself as being a digital producer, data about each and every customer has become precious to me.

User data owned by companies like Google and Facebook can directly translate into their stock prices. This means that data is the determinant of a company's valuation. As data producers, it is imperative for us to think about how to collect big data from customers, process it smartly, and apply it to our business. Not a single event for customers should go to waste by handling it carelessly.

Digital transformation is not restricted to large companies. A small company of twenty employees, like mine, can do it, and everybody can and should also do it as individuals. What changes would digital technology bring to you if you made it a part of yourself? If you own a small restaurant, you should think about which digital technologies you can bring into your business. Imagine the possibilities: Can you use smartphones to take orders? Can you use a chatbot to deal with reservations? What should you do to get big data on customer reviews? Wouldn't it be nice if you can have an AI assistant take calls from your customers instead of having to staff a real person and pay them?

If you are a freelance writer, you need to practice transforming yourself into a one-person digital company. Ask yourself: What should I do to connect myself digitally to the world as a writer? Should I post my latest writings on platforms like Medium? Should I launch a website or blog with WordPress and create a subscription service or an AdSense-based revenue-generating business model? What if I open an Instagram account and post one good quote each day? What technology do I need to learn to make this comprehensive transformation a reality? Should I learn the computer programming language Python and do data crawling to find out which stories people like to hear these days? This is one example of how you can continuously try to integrate digital technology into your business.

The second formula, digital transformation, is the essential requirement for you to make the most out of the first formula, on-tact. No matter how seriously you are willing to connect your skills with digital, you cannot take advantage of the infinite possibilities of digital technology unless you take your first step into the digital world. You can start by putting one "dot" in the digital world instead trying to start with a big picture. Then you can take further steps to learn and master social media skills, websites, and apps that you can use to your advantage.

Digital transformation is not something that you need to understand in the abstract; it is something that you need to experience personally. Just understanding it is not enough to survive in the post-coronavirus world. If I may compare it to immigrating to another country, you can survive and even become successful in that country only when you learn its language and culture. The first thing that you need to do is debut your name in the digital world. Then you can gradually begin using the digital technology that is most useful for you. I hope that digital transformation will become your weapon for life in the new world.

CHAPTER 6

REBOOT FORMULA 3

INDEPENDENT WORKER

It was in early April 2020 that MKTV finally hit the 1 million subscribers mark. The first video I released after hitting the 1 million mark was titled "Spring Club Six-Week Project." In this case, "spring" referred to the helical metal coil, not the season. I named the club "spring" because I wanted to encourage my subscribers to remain resilient and bounce back, like a coiled spring. I wanted to help them find opportunities in the present crisis, instead of feeling constantly weighed down by the coronavirus. During the project, each morning I uploaded a video in which I expressed my thoughts about the coronavirus pandemic and solutions to it. I called on my subscribers to explain their situations in a "comments" box. In this way, we collaborated on ways to overcome the economic recession and crisis by appropriately applying the solutions we came up with.

The day after uploading the first video of the project, I read a comment that reduced me to tears. It had been left by a single-mom subscriber, Esther. She wrote:

> I'm a single mom who barely makes it day to day by trying to build stronger immunity. When it's getting really difficult, I wrap up for the day listening to your motivational speeches. And then…Today, I was told not to come to work anymore. I cried so much on the street. My child is six years old and I usually leave my child at home before I go to work because I cannot send him to a day care at the moment. I hurried home, almost running, because I knew my child was waiting for me to come home after work, and I don't even remember how I got there. I try to remain positive, but that's hard. I really didn't want to break down in front of my child, but when our eyes met, tears just started pouring out. What should I do now?

The situation was already hard enough; she was on her own trying to feed two. I could not imagine how she felt when she had to leave her six-year-old child alone at home in order to make a living. And now that she could not even do that, how devastated she must be. I couldn't think of any words of comfort to give her. I just kept crying.

The coronavirus storm is hitting those who need the most protection. They are targeted most, and they are losing the protective shields that society should have in place for them. The first video garnered many comments, by dozens of people besides Esther, and many of them confided that they had lost their jobs or were afraid they were going to be laid off soon. What could I say to them?

First, I examined the current employment situation facing Koreans. According to some statistics, in March 2020 alone, as many as 1.6 million people were forced to take temporary leave from their jobs, while 467,000 workers lost their jobs in the following month.[18] What will happen to all these people who have been put on temporary leave? Will they ever be able to return to work?

In truth, we already know the answer: many of them won't. Even if they do, they will have little job security. We don't know when social distancing will end, and this crisis could repeat itself at any time in the near future. Businesses have already begun giving jobs to machines, AI, and robots, instead of to humans, in order to survive the crisis. In Gangnam, Seoul, an unmanned café has opened, where customers can order coffee just by pressing a touchpad, without being helped by human employees. Another robot-staffed

---

18 Vladimir Hlasny, "How COVID-19 Wreaked Havoc on South Korea's Labor Market," The Diplomat, August 28, 2020, https://thediplomat.com/2020/08/how-covid-19-wreaked-havoc-on-south-koreas-labor-market/.

café is open twenty-four hours without any human beings on the premises. Even the cosmetic industry saw the launching of a self-service store that operates without any humans to provide service.

Now, we know that on-tact is more than just a digital trend. It is an unavoidable part of our society that we have to accept in order to survive. We may be losing traditional jobs because of digital technology, but the truth is, we all need that technology in order to survive. There is no turning back. If you have already left your job, it might be difficult to return to it. Or it might be impossible because you can be replaced by a machine.

What about those people who remain in their jobs? Is their position secure? In many offices, there is an unsettled feeling. If you are one of those who has a bad feeling about your future, you might not be too far off. Many have seen how lockdowns impact the local and national economy. But it doesn't stop there: even global corporations aren't immune. Take my home country, for example. In the second quarter of 2020, Korea saw the largest quarter-to-quarter drop in exports since 1963.[19] As countries around the world strengthen their protective trade policies, it will be a particularly hard blow to companies that are heavily dependent on exports.

---

19 Troy Stangarone, "COVID-19 Pushes South Korea into Recession," The Diplomat, August 3, 2020, https://thediplomat.com/2020/08/covid-19-pushes-south-korea-into-recession/.

Not long ago, an executive of a well-known stationery company sent me a message on Instagram, asking me to help him promote its products on MKTV. He said that the company had a huge inventory of notebooks piled up in its warehouse. They had been produced for the 2020 school year. Obviously, all schools from elementary to high schools were delaying their opening dates because of the coronavirus, making the notebooks unnecessary. I had never imagined the impact reaching this far. It was at this moment that I realized that untold numbers of companies, in areas that we'd never expected, were struggling. In the future, there could be hundreds of cases in which people will have to worry about the survival of their companies before worrying about saving their jobs.

Since the coronavirus outbreak, I have spent most of my time meeting people. In particular, I met with many CEOs to seek their advice. They were all known to be competent leaders in their industry, with years of experience and accomplishments under their belts. Unfortunately, they were just as lost as I was. I visited them, seeking their advice, but in the course of our conversations, they sought advice from me. One of them had been running a successful business for thirty years, but even he told me that he was out of his depth. He didn't know in which direction to go. It was not because they had any concrete problems, but the rapids that they found themselves in during the crisis were so strong and fast that it was not easy for them to get their bearings.

Large companies that have their own research institutes seem to have noticed what's going on faster than others. In the case of small companies like mine, a crisis like this reverberates through every level. At both the largest and smallest ends of the spectrum, however, it can be easy to make shifts in a timely manner. Large companies have entire research teams to provide insights and instructions. Smaller teams, like mine, can transform themselves faster, since they don't have as many opinions to consider and, therefore, everyone tends to agree very quickly. Companies that have from 100 to 200 employees seem to be the ones that find it most difficult to make fast moves because they are neither small nor big. Their employees are nervous but believe that the size of the company will insulate it from catastrophic events. At every level, employees count on their bosses to do the right thing. But what if their bosses are lost themselves? That's the kind of situation where there is no solution.

At this point, we can draw another conclusion: nobody knows what will happen to the company they are working for at the moment. Let's not count on the boss. Let's count on ourselves instead.

HOW WILL THE CORONAVIRUS CHANGE OUR JOBS?

The most important question facing us now is, in the post-coronavirus world, how can we keep our jobs and how should we work? I can answer that question with one sentence: become an independent worker. Become someone who can "freely and independently" do the work that they want to do, no matter what variables come into play.

An independent worker is someone who doesn't lose a job due to external variables. In life, we often face situations just as unexpected as a global pandemic. It could be your child suddenly getting sick, which requires you to quit your job and care for them. Your husband could lose his job, making you the family's sole breadwinner. Perhaps a business that's been successful suddenly starts declining or closes down altogether due to shifts in consumer demands. All of these could be career ending for someone who is beholden to an organization run by someone else. An independent worker can find work whenever they want, no matter how internal or external circumstances change, and most importantly, they can do it in the way they choose.

Min-jeong has been a web designer for a company for over ten years. Being a talented designer with good sense, she quickly moved up the corporate ladder to become a team leader. Then she got married, had a child, and quit her job in order to care for her newborn. While at home, she started finding work with shopping malls, creating their product detail pages whenever she could find time. After doing this for about a year, she thought it wouldn't be that difficult for her to create her own shopping mall.

Min-jeong said, "Illustrating has always been my hobby. So, just for fun, I showcased some of my illustrations on Instagram, and people said that if they were available on posters, they would buy them in a heartbeat. I was not a stranger to the online shopping mall business because I've been creating product detail pages for a while. So I just gave it a try without thinking about it. I used my illustrations to create art posters, and they sold well. I made fairly good money from them because, other than my time and effort, it didn't cost me much to make them."

A short while later, a company reached out to her and asked her to help them build and launch an online shopping mall. The company told her that she had just the talent they were looking for—with her ability to combine design, marketing, and information important to the shopper. In the end, Min-jeong made the decision to work part time for the company, designing its product detail pages and Instagram promotions. She had the freedom to manage her own time, only attending meetings when absolutely necessary. And she also kept running her own online shopping mall, while working for this company. A short while ago, the company offered her a full-time position as a team leader.

She explained, "I was asked to join the company and work full-time, in charge of the design team. I'm considering accepting the offer and working as an in-house designer, maybe just for two years. My child is old enough to go to a day care center, and the salary is good, too. I will be able to learn and keep pace with industry trends as well. After that, I'll think about what to do next."

How would you define Min-jeong in terms of the work she does for a living? Is she a self-employed owner of an online shopping mall? Or is she a freelancer because she's working for a shopping mall under contract? Or is she a full-time employee because she is now going to work for a company? If you asked me, I would say that she is a truly independent worker.

Min-jeong's living situation changed several times throughout her working-from-home journey, but she never stopped working. She has been doing what she wanted to do, despite changes in her environment. During this process, she was able to hone her craft, acquire more-diverse skills, and significantly increase her income. Whether she works on a full-time or part-time basis is not important. What matters is that she can accept or decline a request from a company at any time, depending on what fits into her schedule. What matters to Min-jeong is having a position that allows her to work flexible hours, while doing what she does best. Experts predict that in the next two to three years, we will see the coming of a world of independent workers, with similar qualifications and backgrounds. According to them, a trend that had slowly been moving in a certain direction has now progressed at an accelerated speed because of the coronavirus.

Flexible forms of work–such as flexible work-hour arrangements and working from home–have previously been attempted mostly by IT companies. These forms of working have been a choice in the past, but now social distancing mandates have changed it from a matter of choice to a matter of necessity. It's essentially a standard now. Twitter CEO Jack Dorsey announced to his employees in May 2020 that they can work from home "forever," if they want to.[20] In the past, the general idea was that employees had to be working together, within the same confined space, for efficient and speedy communication. But we now see that it is possible to achieve efficient and speedy communication even if we don't work in the same, conventional way that we used to.

The shift to flexible forms of working has also given companies a broader range of options. In the past, when hiring new employees, one of companies' job requirements was that they were able to commute to work. Companies would not hire job candidates who could not come to work every day, no matter how skilled and talented they were. But companies now hire people whom they hesitated to hire in the past because they lived too far from work. They will also negotiate flexible work hours for people like Min-jeong, who have kids and have to stay home to raise them. That means that the way we work is growing more diversified

---

20 Heather Kelly, "Twitter Employees Don't Ever Have to Go Back to the Office (unless They Want To)," *The Washington Post*, May 13, 2020, https://www.washingtonpost.com/technology/2020/05/12/twitter-work-home/.

and flexible than ever. It also means that the optimal time for independent workers is coming.

THE LIFE THAT MILLENNIALS REALLY WANT

For members of the millennial generation, who value work-life balance, the independent workers' world is ideal. Millennials–those who were born between the early 1980s and the mid-1990s–have always struggled between building the life that they want and supporting themselves. Their pursuit of dreams and happiness is fine, but they cannot give up their job security for either. Therefore, they stay in a job in order to make a living, but their minds are on the after-work activities that they enjoy. Since both job and outside activities are important to them, work-life balance is an important issue for them. They have to straddle precariously between work and life. The changes happening now are good news for them.

Kim Yong-seop, author of *Un-contact* and director of the Sharp Imagination Institute, explained that millennials are happy to work from home because they are familiar with noncontact:

> Working from home instead of going to work is what millennials have always wanted, because they can win in the job market with their skills alone, without having to suck up to their superiors or walk on eggshells around the boss.

It will become the grand trend in the job market when millennials enter it in full swing.

What will happen if on-tact becomes our standard routine in the post-coronavirus world? What will the world look like if everyone works from home rather than commuting for a nine-to-five job? When this new generation, with its new solutions, dominates the workplace, workplace culture and values as we know them, as well as the office job as we know it, will gradually become a thing of the past.

We also need to pay close attention to the criteria that millennials use when choosing a job. They make choices for different reasons than those of previous generations for whom it didn't matter if a certain job was what they wanted. Previous generations looked for jobs that would keep them out of poverty; it was enough for them to get a college degree and a job that paid well. Millennials, on the other hand, think about their jobs in terms of the lifestyle it can provide them with.

Millennials are different: even if they find a job at a company they like, they don't hesitate to quit that job if it doesn't meet their criteria for living. Their parents are flabbergasted when they find out that their millennial children have quit a good job, but for millennials themselves, satisfying both "how I want to live" and "what I do for living" is the basis of their self-esteem. Maybe this is the right way of life. Those who dare to take up the challenge that older generations have failed to meet are what I call independent workers.

But it is not easy to become an independent worker. There is only one thing that can fill the gap left by contact: skill. Until now, there were many things that you could substitute for skill. Your job performance may have been less than perfect, but still you were considered a good employee if you had good interpersonal relationships and proved yourself loyal to the company. But if the space where you worked with others is gone, the only things that remain and sustain you are your performance and skill. Therefore, you must ask yourself this question: "Am I recognized just as much for my skill when I work on my own as I was when I worked with others in an office?"

If you are a skilled, competent talent, you will have the opportunity to break through even the thick wall of a prestigious academic degree. As of 2018, half of Apple's employees in the United States did not have a college degree. Isn't that shocking? Apple is a company that receives job applications from the world's top talents, but half of the company's employees have a high school diploma or less. This means that Apple hires competent people, regardless of their academic background. And Apple is not alone. This is a universal trend being seen across the digital industry.

Not long ago, our company hired a new producer, Yoon-jeong. She is a forty-year-old single mother, hired after fierce competition for the job. Yoon-jeong had participated in an educational project designed to train single mothers to become video editors at Grow Mom, a foundation that I founded to help and support single mothers. She had received a month-long internship at MKTV and was able to complete it when the director in charge of our YouTube team came to me and said, "Yoon-jeong clearly has a good understanding of video content, and she's good at writing subtitles. She also has a good sense of design. She is much better than those who majored in video in college."

The director was the kind of person who did everything by the book and never said something that he didn't mean. Besides, while hiring and working with employees, I myself realized how video-editing skills really had nothing to do with a college degree. Those who graduated from college with a degree in video production knew how to handle basic equipment but had to be taught the basics because they didn't have actual work experience. There was not much difference between those who had studied for four years in college and those who had studied only six months at a vocational school. It wasn't a college degree that determined a person's competency: it was the effort and passion with which a person tried to be good at the job.

Yoon-jeong joined our company simply because of her talents. She had applied to participate in the Grow Mom project by chance. For several months, she practiced and honed her skills at a private vocational school. When she realized that she had a special talent, she secured a job through her diligent work and passion. Is it just luck that strikes those like Yoon-jeong? No, it isn't. When one door closes, another door is sure to open. Ultimately, this is what I want to tell Esther, the YouTube commenter, as well.

Instead of feeling sorry for yourself, standing before a closed door, open another door for yourself. We are about to enter a time when you can win with your skill alone, even if you don't have an impressive degree, connections, or past career experience. A world where you can work of your own accord, when you want, and as much as you want, is on the horizon. My suggestion is that you become an independent worker as soon as possible. Build a skill that is yours and that cannot be replaced by anyone else, and use it to find a wonderful life.

FIVE QUALIFICATIONS THAT AN INDEPENDENT WORKER MUST HAVE

To be most helpful to Esther and to all readers of this book who are interested in becoming an independent worker, I've compiled the five essential steps you must take. As a business owner, these are what I see as critical for succeeding in the post-coronavirus world.

1. DEVELOP CORE CONTENT FOR YOURSELF AND YOUR BUSINESS

Core content is whatever you cannot live without. If there's something that you are interested in—a passion that you never tire of, no matter how much time you spend on it—that something is very likely to be your core content. You might be good at dancing or cooking, or you might find math a fun subject. You might have marketing ideas popping up in your head daily, or maybe you can ride a bike better than most others. Or you might draw cartoons well, play games well, or organize well. You might be good at one thing or multiple things. Use them all to your advantage.

The core content that you identify is what you will work to master: the skill that you will use to become an independent worker. You must believe that you can do it differently than others who have come before you. Once you feel confident about your competency at your core-content skill, you can begin to do your own marketing in order to make yourself known in the industry of your choice. You can make a living on your own once your core content begins to attract attention. If you can gradually add social influence to it, you can even help others, and thanks to it, you can live a life filled with self-esteem.

What's important is concentrating on what you do with joy or passion for a long time before you become a competent independent worker. Work and life must become one in order for you to have higher efficiency during this time of concentration. You have a better chance of succeeding as an independent worker only when "how you want to live" is in line with "what you want to do." You can't grow independently if you are unwilling to invest your time in what you do and are tempted to quit because the work bores you.

2. DIGITAL TECHNOLOGY IS THE FOUNDATION

Independent workers usually start out alone. Not only do they have to be masters of their work, but they also have to promote themselves, manage their customers, and develop their careers—all by themselves. Everything from social media marketing to specific promotions is handled independently. Since I started working professionally, I have learned a variety of digital work skills: word processing, PowerPoint, video production, blogging, online communities, forums, YouTube, Instagram marketing, Facebook ad management, website building, and app development. Each time a new platform was launched, I immediately learned how to use it, and now I can identify the connection and timeliness of all these platforms and immediately apply what I find to what I do. When you are an independent worker, it is a basic requirement that you build a system that allows you to work regardless of where you are located. Create a platform where you can promote yourself anywhere in the world and do all necessary work with competency.

3. CREATE A SELF-UPGRADE SYSTEM

I study constantly. Having core content in your field means that you must reorganize and upgrade it every day. You need to have at least three to five upgrade systems. You can maintain the core content and even make it more competitive only when you study all other areas relevant to that core content. Only then can you come up with creative ideas. Especially in this fast-paced time, you can quickly fall behind others in just six months if you stay unfocused and get sidetracked. Being an independent worker may sound cool, but the truth is that it is more labor intensive than you think. The pain from that labor doesn't bother you much because you are doing what you like to do.

As an independent worker, you can achieve self-growth only when you invest in what you do. You must invest in yourself or your future work by managing your money well, even if it's just a small amount. An independent worker is a small company in itself, and there is no future for a company that doesn't invest.

You must use about 30 percent of the money you make to study for the future. In my case, I continually study English, digital technology, read books, study science, and engage in my hobbies every day. Others ask me if it doesn't tire me out, but I'm fine with it. You must be able to tell what tires you and what keeps you busy. Keeping yourself busy is better than having too much spare time, and having a lot of work is better than being sad because you have none. That's what I've personally experienced during my many years of being an independent worker.

When the tiring times of hard work pass, my career and I are better for them. How great it is because when I share with others the results of my efforts, I make money, and I also build my career!

4. BUILD AND MAINTAIN YOUR NETWORK

When working independently, there often comes a time when you have no work. You get flustered when you have no idea why you stopped getting job orders. This is the hardest moment for independent workers. When it happens, you should not keep asking yourself why. If you keep asking the question, you start blaming and reproaching yourself, and before you know it, you develop depression. In the worst-case scenario, you feel so isolated and defeated that it can bring you down completely.

My son, who is studying music, explained it so clearly to me recently. He said, "Mom, do you know what musicians need to be most mindful of? Getting along with older musicians. Freelancers might look like they work on their own, but it is rare for them to make it that way because they all need to be introduced to others and recommend one another. You need to be introduced in the industry before you can take your first step. So these days, I've been going out with older musicians to eat, drink, and talk with them."

My son is fresh out of college and just started working in the music business, and he is an independent worker. Alone at home, he writes songs and plays the piano. Of course, he sells the music that he writes, but he makes money mostly by playing music. What if my son becomes isolated in this business? He'll run out of money, his skills will start getting rusty, and eventually, he will be forced to forget about working independently. If you think that an independent worker is somebody who works alone, you're wrong. You work independently, but you must also make sure that you keep growing by staying closely connected with people and society. This is where some of the on-tact strategies that I shared in Reboot Formula 1 can come in handy.

5. BE SMART ABOUT MANAGING YOUR MONEY

I've known many independent workers, but a fair number of them are sloppy when it comes to money management. They are so focused on doing the work that they like to do that they often get into a situation where they can hardly support themselves. But you can work only when you have all the necessities of living. If you want to continuously support your dream, you must be smart with your finances.

I have a friend who is a designer. He makes money on every

job order, but there are times when he doesn't have any work and therefore doesn't make any money. Job orders can stop once every while, but humans cannot live without a steady and stable supply of food. His problem is that when he gets paid and has money, he goes out to meet friends and buys them drinks, buys whatever he wants, and keeps spending money until it runs out. He remains broke until the next job order comes in. And this routine keeps repeating. Living this way, it's obvious that he has no future. We had a talk, and he confided, "Listening to you, I realize that I was not an independent worker. I was just a lifelong part-timer."

The answer to his problem lies in what he said. He created his own unstable situation by repeating the same routine of spending money when he has money and going broke when money stops coming in. You must learn how to save money whenever you make any and how to manage yourself and the people around you to ensure steady job orders. You are a true independent worker only when you become financially independent.

I think that my employees are all staying with me because, ultimately, staying with this company gives them the answers they need about how to live their life. They can learn and gain experience for a while, make money, prepare to start their own business, or remain in the company to grow it together and share the fruit. I believe that the answers that they find will take them to the next step, where tomorrow is better than today. For that reason, my company gives diplomas to employees when they leave the company. This is meant to tell them that leaving the company is equivalent to graduating and moving to the next step. The diploma signifies our sincere cheering for them to have a wonderful new start in whatever their next step takes them to.

If you must leave your current company or if your company closes due to coronavirus, give yourself three days to work through your reactions. Then rise up courageously and give yourself a graduation certificate. Compliment yourself for all your hard work and encourage yourself. Get yourself admitted to a new world as an independent worker.

We will have to endure this time of crisis for the next several years. It is possible that you will come to a moment when your "work" itself collapses. When it happens, don't forget the third Reboot Formula, which is becoming an independent worker. To ensure that you do it, you must remember to tell yourself this: "Work may disappear, but I am still here."

Pull yourself together and courageously reboot yourself to become an independent worker.

CHAPTER 7

```
┌────────────────────┐
│ ▌▌▌▌▌▌▌▌▌          │
└────────────────────┘
```

REBOOT FORMULA 4

SAFETY

For several years, I've been traveling with my oldest daughter, just the two of us. Usually, my daughter picks the destination. This mother-daughter traveling started when my daughter started making money. Watching her paying for my flight tickets, I enjoyed the pleasant sense of reward for having raised a successful child. But this generous treatment from my daughter didn't last long. Toward the end of January, when the coronavirus situation was growing serious, my daughter asked me, with a disappointed look on her face, "Mom, it's not going to work out this year, is it?"

I answered honestly. I said, "I don't think so. Even if there are flights available, we cannot travel this year because we don't have the money. I don't even have any speeches scheduled, and where would we go at a time like this?" These days, however, I couldn't dream of traveling overseas, even if I had the money. We might have to stash our passports away in the drawer for one or two years.

One day, I was talking with my employees and asked them how they thought people would travel abroad.

"I guess people might feel nervous about sitting so close to other passengers in the economy section like they did in the past. I think passengers might want to have at least one empty seat in between."

"People would check-in online in advance instead of standing in line at the airport."

"I wouldn't feel safe to touch the check-in machine that so many other people have touched. I wish airports would introduce touchless machines."

"Worst of all, you would be so screwed if you traveled to another country and were confirmed to have the virus there. I think I would not travel unless the travel agency guarantees that they'll connect me to a local hospital when I'm suspected to have the coronavirus."

"Well, don't you think all travelers should buy coronavirus insurance before going on a trip?"

"Gee, this is getting too complicated. I would say, just don't travel overseas. Just travel to Jeju Island. Why bother to travel to other countries when Korea is the safest of all."

We talked about it for a while, but in the end, our conclusions were Jeju Island and safety.

With the coronavirus outbreak, safety is the most important prerequisite for anything you do. People shouldn't even attempt to do anything unless the concern over contagion is resolved. These days, people are doubtful about going anywhere. They ask, "Is that place okay? Are you sure it's safe there?"

This is the kind of question that nobody even thought about until just a year ago. In the past, everyone asked questions like, "Is it cheap there? Is the food delicious there? Is that movie good? Is it fun? Is the service good? Does it have a good view?"

But now, no matter how cheap or how much you get for the money you pay, nobody even bothers to go anywhere unless it's safe. It is because "safety" has become the criterion for consumption and the most important prerequisite. If you own a business and you cannot say confidently that your business ensures safety, you might as well just close down now. Since the coronavirus pandemic, human desires all depend on one issue: safety from the virus.

SAFETY CONSCIOUSNESS SAVED KOREA

When the crisis hit, Korea's response to the pandemic–commonly referred to as K-quarantine–became a role model around the world. Korean-made virus diagnostic kits are in such high demand that manufacturers cannot keep up. Then Korea implemented the world's first drive-through test checkpoints. It takes only ten minutes to get tested for coronavirus with the drive-through system, which allows people to get tested without having to get out of their cars, as they would when ordering from Starbucks and McDonald's. The biggest benefit of this system is that it doesn't require disinfectant procedures before taking the test, which minimizes both the contact between drivers and medical staff and the time between tests. Sam Kim, a Bloomberg News reporter, commented that this system proved that Korea is "among the world's most innovative country [sic]."[21]

More than anything, the biggest asset that Korea has gained from this experience is "national credibility." Korea succeeded in containing the spread of coronavirus without going to a lockdown, and not only that, the trust between the government and the Korean people has made a big impression on people in other countries. Bill Gates showed a keen interest in Korea's preventive measures against the pandemic. He couldn't praise the country enough, and his foundation contributed $4.83 million to Korea Telecom's

---

21 Sam Kim, Twitter Post, February 26, 2020, 1:45 a.m., https://twitter.com/samkimasia/status/1232557316886523904.

research on a predictive model for infectious diseases.[22] This is just one example of what the asset of trust can do. Suppose the United States has to import a product from another country. From which country do you think the United States will import that product: a country that has shady data on infectious disease, no proper diagnostic measures, and no transparency, or would the United States import it from a country that is transparent and reliable?

Recently, I saw a public service advertisement on CNN. In the ad, a man goes grocery shopping at a supermarket and brings the bags home. He wears plastic gloves even after washing his hands. He then wipes with disinfectant wet tissues the packages of all the products he bought, including shampoo, tissues, and cereal. He even goes on to wipe and clean the table where he placed the grocery bags. The ad ends with this line: Stay safe.

Most of the products sold in the United States are imported. Of course, as time goes by, the anxiety over the coronavirus will subside. But people will remain conscious of safety issues, and countries will want to trade with "safe countries" that have proven records of transparency and reliability. Even as of now, many countries are hesitating to open their doors to foreign visitors, mainly because there is no guarantee of

---

22 Pulse Media Group, "KT to Come Up with Self-Diagnosis App to Detect Virus Infection within the Year," Pulse Media Group, May 25, 2020, https://pulsenews.co.kr/view. php?year=2020&no=534142.

safety. Each country will campaign to let other countries know how safe it is, and other countries will try to verify how safe a certain country is before doing any business with that country. In that regard, having been acknowledged as a country that succeeded in preventing the spread of the virus, Korea has given other countries around the world the impression that it is a "safe country." That means that Korea has acquired a highly value-added label that reads "safety."

On the other hand, Europe, the United States, Japan, and many other countries that we believed were advanced countries are struggling futilely with the coronavirus. There were countries that were unable to get even an accurate number of confirmed cases, due to the delay in large-scale testing, and there were countries that nearly panicked because they couldn't get hold of enough test kits. In many parts of the world, hospitals were not equipped to accommodate the waves of confirmed patients rushing in, and many patients were neglected. The fever of panic buying resulted in many products running out, and governments and people clashed in psychological warfare over the mandatory use of masks. In the end, the United States and European countries enforced the ultimate measure of "shutting down." The shutdown brought entire countries to a stop.

So the question is, what made this difference? It could be Korea's system and technological power, but I believe that Korea could be ahead of others because Koreans had "safety consciousness." Koreans believed that ensuring the safety of the people was the top priority. That top priority was to be protected at all costs.

The coronavirus crisis hit Japan around the same time as it hit Korea, and Japan also declared that the safety of the people was its top priority. But in reality, it wasn't. The Japanese government valued the Olympic Games and the massive economic gain that they could get from hosting them more than it was concerned with the consequences of the coronavirus. As a result, Japan lost its golden opportunity and fell into the coronavirus trap. Ultimately, Korea became the most successful country in the world to control the coronavirus crisis. The choice that Koreans made, even if it required loss and sacrifice, ended up saving Korea and its being acknowledged as an advanced country when it came to safety.

SAFETY VIEWED FROM AN ECONOMIC PERSPECTIVE

While comparing Korea and other countries, I learned two painfully clear lessons. The first is that safety will be the standard and prerequisite of everything that we do in the future. Additionally, ensuring safety is easier said than done. Safety does not come free. Breaking free from all conventional methods requires firm determination and willingness to take loss and sacrifice. Of course, it costs money for individuals or companies to implement disinfecting and other preventive measures. You might have to close your business for a while to do it, or you might have to spend money to purchase new equipment. Therefore, you need to have a firm determination to guarantee safety at any cost or investment.

Until now, safety did not seem to have anything to do with immediate gain. It was a constraint and a duty that was mandated by laws and regulations. But going forward, it will be different. Now safety must be viewed from an economic perspective. You can prevent further losses and create added value in the future only when you invest in safety without hesitation—even if you must swallow some losses in the beginning.

US retailers, such as Amazon, are investing a massive amount of money to create a "robot chain." They plan to create a logistics chain that runs from the first manufacturing process to the last delivery process. Instead of humans, they will use only robots and digital technology, out of concern that coronavirus could stay alive on the surface of products or that packages or people might get infected during the delivery process. According to the robot industry, orders for robots are still pouring in even though we are in a recession. This indicates that even though companies are being forced to tighten their belts, they aren't sparing anything when it comes to investing in robots. It will not be long before we see robots leaving packages at our doors. This will rapidly become a reality because our survival depends on it.

This is not just happening in the retail industry. Safety technologies are being developed and introduced everywhere. Elevators became one of the riskiest spaces in the wake of the coronavirus pandemic. Recently, however, a technology has been introduced that allows you to use control buttons without touching them; instead, they detect the temperature of your hand. It will take a while to see this technology installed in the elevators of my apartment building, but I'm sure that going forward, elevators with built-in touchless buttons will be installed in every new building. Since facial-recognition gates have also been developed, it is certain that similar technologies will be developed and introduced at an accelerating speed to ensure our safety by minimizing contact and contagion as much as possible.

"Safety" is an essential adjective that in the future will be added to just about every area: safe schools, safe travel, safe food, safe products, and so forth. If your business is not safe and you cannot assure your customers of their safety, you have no chance of bringing your business back to life again. "Smart safety" is the technology that keeps people safe and the technology that will make your business keep moving forward. Safety has not been a part of the technologies born during the fourth industrial revolution, and it is a category that we have added to it with a sense of urgency in order to survive. Going forward, safety will become a new technology that reigns over everything, and quick-thinking companies are already investing in it without regard to the dollar figure.

Now we must include the element of safety in every product and service, from the planning stage to production. Companies that applied this change early on are enjoying a coronavirus-induced business boom right now. In response to the growing awareness of hygiene, antibacterial features that suppress the breeding and spreading of bacteria and viruses are becoming important, even when choosing construction materials. Reflecting this trend, in 2018 Dongkuk Steel debuted and started selling a product called Luxteel Bio, which is an antibacterial, colored steel plate, and it has been receiving numerous orders from abroad.[23] This is a good example of companies that are thriving because of the coronavirus. All these changes indicate that we have entered an era where highly safety-oriented products are acknowledged as high-end brands in the market.

ARE YOUR SERVICES AND MARKETING PREPARED?

Even in a service industry, you need to practice passing your business through the safety filter. When it comes to safety, service has to be combined with the previously explained on-tact. Large shopping malls and department stores are the hardest hit by the coronavirus. Department stores suffered a massive 70–90 percent drop in sales. Lotte, a Korean retail conglomerate, started to turn its business into online

---

23   Michael Herh, "Dongkuk Steel's Luxteel Bio Draws Attention amid Spread of COVID-19," Business Korea, February 25, 2020, http://www.businesskorea.co.kr/news/articleView. html?idxno=41810.

distribution by closing 120 supermarkets, department stores, and off-line stores, including sixteen large marts, in 2020.[24] There is no other choice for the company but to go online if they want to survive by bringing back female customers whose top priority is safety.

The owner of Vainer, a luxury shoe brand that is popular among middle-aged to senior female customers, recently called me and asked for my help. He said, "A big chunk of our sales comes from department stores, but now that customers have stopped coming to department stores, inventory is piling up in our warehouse. It breaks my heart each time I look at the inventory, and I don't know where I'll find the money to pay my employees. Can you give me an idea what to do?"

Vainer is a company that boasts a massive customer base consisting of elderly mothers, who became the company's devoted fans because it has been putting on nationwide festivals for aged mothers each year. But now that these mothers have stopped going out, the company has recorded a 90 percent drop in sales. After having a talk with the owner, it was decided that we should have a special live show on MKTV to sell Vainer shoes at discounted prices. Many mothers were not in the habit of using credit cards to make online purchases, but we ended up selling 4,000 pairs

24   Kyongae Choi, "Lotte Shopping to Sell 121 Stores This Year due to Virus Impact," Yonhap News, May 24, 2020, https://en.yna.co.kr/view/AEN20200524001400320.

of shoes by pitching their children to buy those luxury shoes as Mother's Day gifts. We ultimately reached the sales goal, but I was more concerned about the future of his business.

I told him, "This live show worked out fine, but it was only a short-term solution. It isn't reasonable to expect mothers to come to stores to shop anytime soon. And it will also be difficult for you to hold a nationwide festival for mothers the way you've been doing for years. That said, you know that mothers in their sixties and seventies watch YouTube videos these days. How about using these mothers as your models and making a video of them wearing your shoes? And taking orders by phone. I think that's the solution for you to pull through this crisis."

If you fail to come up with a safe and comfortable way for customers to purchase your products, it will be difficult to survive in the post-coronavirus world. Wouldn't it be unfortunate if a promising brand such as Vainer failed to adopt an on-tact solution and ended up failing? You must drop all the usual services that used to work in the past. Let go of the previous marketing approaches as well. If you cannot guarantee safety, it will be impossible to bring any customers to your business.

Safe marketing will become an increasingly important consideration. It is important to make sure that your customers fully understand how safety conscious you are in every part of your marketing. Companies need to reassure consumers by disclosing all information about their products, such as ingredients or country of origin, as transparently as possible. Companies should also emphasize that their products are safe so that customers trust them and buy their products. They also need to market through compelling storytelling, by using photos, videos, and detailed explanations. And they need to improve their reputation for safety and reliability by providing eco-friendly products and services.

E-commerce is an area that is enjoying a boom due to the coronavirus. But there are many customers who are not happy about e-commerce companies using excessive amounts of materials for packaging. Indiscriminate use of disposable materials, such as plastic bags, Styrofoam, and paper boxes go against the awareness of the environment that the coronavirus has raised. In response, the online delivery company Coupang provided customers with an eco-friendly, reusable cooler bag called Fresh Bag, and Shinsegae's online shopping mall, SSG, also introduced the I'll Be Bag that customers can reuse almost indefinitely.

Customers' awareness of safety may be evolving faster than that of product manufacturers. According to a survey conducted by the global consulting firm Kearney in April 2020, 83 percent of the respondents said that they consider environmental impacts at least occasionally when making a purchase decision, representing "a permanent shift toward environmental products and services." Kearney concluded that "the heightened awareness between the close, and perilous, relationship between human beings and nature, underscored by the current pandemic, has made consumers even more committed to doing better in addressing environmental issues."[25]

If you own a restaurant, you should think about operating safely every day. In addition, you need to come up with a strategy to make your customers recognize that yours is a safe restaurant. Be it a safe after-school academy, safe library, safe dry cleaner, or safe convenience store, your business will survive only when its name is preceded by the key adjective "safe."

Now that the turbulence is settling in some parts of the world, we can relax a little. Consumer behaviors, which have been frozen in time, are now being revitalized. Stores that have been closed are now opening their doors and getting ready to welcome customers again. Time that had paused for a while has started moving again, and the post-coronavirus world is emerging. At this point, safety is something that we must think about seriously and be prepared for.

25 Greg Portal, Corey Chafin, and Christina Carlson, "Consumer Support Still Strong as Earth Day Celebrates Its 50th Birthday," A. T. Kearney, Inc., accessed February 11, 2021, https://www.kearney.com/documents/20152/14815893/ Consumer+support+still+strong+as+Earth+Day+celebrates+its+50th+birthday. pdf/48a20e8a-1d7c-2b2f-06d6-451064e6ecec?t=1590590289205.

In the changed world, safety is a key issue and a yardstick that will determine the success or failure of your business. You should use all your imagination to set up your business so that it will not go down the drain just because it failed to pass through the important safety filter. It goes without saying that you must communicate with your customers with sincerity, and the outcome of the communication must be as beautiful as it can be. If there is a secret to successfully finding answers to a problem that you encounter for the first time, it is sincerity. Wholehearted, sincere dedication to safety will complete your reboot.

PART 3

WRITE YOUR LIFESAVING "REBOOT SCENARIO"

To reboot to fit into a new era, you must clear out all the outdated practices that you have been holding on to.

It's about parting with your old ways that have served their purpose. Within the basic framework of your business, you must replace them with new ideas, new roles, and new methods in order to save your job, your money, your family, and even your future.

You can be reborn as a competent businessperson only when you change everything.

CHAPTER 8

TURN ON THE ENGINE AND REBOOT

"Mom, is studying that much fun? You've been studying for months!"

That's what my children cry out to me every night. I have been so busy studying about the post-coronavirus world that I hardly spend time on anything else. Since they were little, my children have thought of me as not so much their mom but rather as "a vehicle running with a built-in engine." That is understandable, considering how much I work, both professionally and in my personal life. But in the past few years, I've lost power and started slowing down. Every day, I made speeches and met different people in different venues, but somehow I was dragging. One day, I was on my way home from a speech event in a local city when it suddenly hit me: When I get older and can't make speeches anymore, I'll have to bring all my employees together and tell them we must say goodbye to each other. Then, as I continue to grow older, I will spend my time traveling, which I haven't been able to do.

I could see a predictable future before my eyes. When I thought about how I was moving toward it, I could not find the energy to be excited. Then, when I thought how the coronavirus was forging a new order, I suddenly felt energy surging within me. I wanted to play in the new game, and I felt I could make a new dream come true in the process. It seemed I wasn't the only one who was running. Lately, companies have started running forward again, while completely revamping their existing businesses.

According to a stock expert whom I met, stock prices are expected to rally around the world over the next ten years. For the past thirty years, since personal computers were introduced, the global economy has been losing its growth momentum, consequently causing a prolonged economic slump. Some people point out that the economic slump would have been greater and lasted longer had there not been the new market of China. He predicted that the coronavirus would accelerate the advent of the future to a world that has been slowly dying, and the fourth industrial revolution would provide us with a new growth engine that would make the economy start growing again.

Some people will grow as independent workers, some will

move up the ladder by playing the game with the safety card, and some will expand businesses by applying the on-tact and digital transformation formulas. And some companies will resolve business issues and achieve rapid growth by applying all four formulas to their businesses.

It will be like what happened in America, a country where people came in droves in search of new opportunities and achieved tremendous growth by lavishly investing in technologies and resources. People's desire to seize opportunities when a new system was being established in an uncharted land is what gave birth to the American dream as we know it. In everything, a new start is always teeming with new opportunities.

The future that is approaching us at an accelerated speed at the moment is another New World. We're trying to create things that we have never had before, and we are making attempts that we had never attempted before. On-tact opened the world of telemedicine, online education, and video conferences, and digital technology is integrating artificial intelligence, robots, big data, and 5G communication. People are transforming themselves into independent workers and offering their skills for hire. We are joining together to safeguard our generation as well as those after us. The post-coronavirus world is similar to the New World. How many talents and partners will this new world require? The world is looking for people who can run forward in the same direction, while sharing the same vision.

If changes frighten you, it is impossible for you to accept them in your daily life, much less find opportunities to use them to leap forward. We may have forgotten our dreams for a while because we've been overwhelmed with busy daily lives, but in order to enter the huge order forged out of chaos, we need to reconfirm our dreams.

MAKE REBOOT FORMULAS INTO MATERIALS FOR YOUR DREAMS

I've always thought that I was interacting with my dream, rather than chasing it. I reached my dream of becoming the best motivational speaker by diligently studying and preparing myself to make good speeches. Dreams are like living creatures: they need to be learned, trusted, and given opportunities to evolve based on the external environment. Then my dreams can grow and make a decent human out of me.

As the world began changing faster than ever, I started teaching my dreams about the speed, direction, and ways of these changes as I always have. Dreams will grow while feeding on the materials that I give them and help me become a more decent person than before. Changes don't just take away what is mine. They sometimes make the link between me and my dreams stronger. There are three effects that the changes happening in the world are having on my dreams.

THE PRESENT MAY CHANGE THE DIRECTION OF YOUR DREAMS

Even in the past, I had to know the world inside out in order to find the right direction for my dreams. I had to know where the world was headed, which industry was declining or growing, where I should go to have my ability recognized, and which job group was in high demand. Anticipating changes is essential to pointing your dreams in the right direction. If you are not sure what kind of job you should have in the future, use the Reboot Formulas to help you clarify your dreams. Stay open to change, remembering that your dreams need to evolve with the times.

THE PRESENT WILL AFFECT THE WAY YOU CHASE YOUR DREAMS

Even if the direction of your dreams remains the same, the path you take to accomplish them will likely change completely. You may find yourself wondering what you need to study to realize your dreams, what jobs you should take while you work toward your dreams, whether you can work independently or not. The dream-chasing method that leads you to success may not have been available when you began on your path.

Suppose someone's passion is editing music and animation, which they have been doing at home. They doubt that such activities would ever be of interest to others, but when they combine on-tact, digital technology, and independence with their passion, they become convinced that their activities could turn into a dream job. In the past, they felt depressed when they met friends who were employed by companies because they felt that they were falling behind those others. But in a new world and a new context, they can become proud of themselves while doing their own work from home. They have the confidence that they are chasing their dreams one step at a time and believe that they have a wonderful job.

The way you chase your dreams will become more flexible and diverse. There will come a world where such diverse dreams will be respected. Those who dream new dreams will grab more attention than those who struggle to meet the outside world's standards. A new era has opened in which you can proudly move forward to realize your dreams, no matter how trivial or eccentric it may be.

CHANGES HAPPENING NOW WILL CHANGE YOU AND YOUR LIFE

Once you determine the direction of your dreams and come up with dream-chasing strategies, your identity also changes. In the past, many people dreamed of making a lot of money and becoming successful but had to give up their dreams because they were constrained in so many ways. It was a world that was not generous to people–a world where numerous factors predetermined whether you could become successful and make a lot of money: you were too old, had children to care for, or didn't have an impressive degree. For example, many stay-at-home mothers could not find a job because they could not commute to an office. Their dream was simply inaccessible to them.

But today, doors are wide open for you to succeed as long as you are competent, even if you are old, have to care for a child, or don't have a degree. You don't have to work for a company. You can realize your dreams as long as they are realistic and you dedicate yourself to the Reboot Formulas. Once all the hurdles and obstacles are gone, you'll become confident that you can make it. It will be as though all the energies that fuel your life are changing. For those who know how to use changes to their advantage, the post-coronavirus world will bring life-changing opportunities.

CHOOSE THE POSITIVE INSTEAD OF THE NEGATIVE

The world in which we live is constantly changing, and we must change to adapt to those changes. Until now, the changes were happening slowly enough that we could keep up with them. We didn't have to rack our brains and desperately search for ways to make a living because we just needed to benchmark what others had achieved or get one more professional license.

But post-pandemic changes are different. The order of the world has been completely transformed. You cannot guarantee that you will keep anything–be it your job or just your daily routine–if you don't know how to apply the change formulas. Using the Reboot Formulas, you can maintain the life you want by acquiring the skills you need to solve the problems that you face in today's world. You can successfully move into the new world and completely transform yourself by keeping only the basic framework of your occupation and changing everything else.

Until now, the key to self-development that we have pursued has been additive. Self-development was all about diligently studying what the world was demanding and building up our knowledge one layer after another. For that reason, diligent career men and women attended reading clubs after work or studied English on their way to work in the morning. It was considered a good way to develop themselves, get more qualifications under their belts, and be able to compete successfully for jobs.

Post-coronavirus, however, the key to self-development will be removal. Many of the skills that we used in the contact and analog world have become useless assets. What we need now is to abandon these useless skills to make room for new, more-relevant ones. You can bring in new skills only when you discard those that are no longer useful.

There are many who rationally understand the need for change but hesitate to change themselves. They have trouble letting go of what they have. Companies can quickly clear out their physical inventory, but for individuals, it is difficult to clear out mental inventory. It is unsettling for them to think how the things that have been supporting their lives are about to disappear, and it is even more devastating because they equate it with losing a part of their own existence. But inventory is just what it is: inventory, not identity. If you have assets that used to be your lifeline but now are no longer useful, you must clear them out quickly. You can invest in something new only when the old inventory is cleared out. You can make a profit if you sell something worth $100 for just $20 and invest that $20 to make it to grow to $200.

Those who understand what the new order will be in the post-coronavirus world are quick to choose and focus. They know what basic values they must retain, what to throw away, and what to grab. On the other hand, those who are slow to recognize the changes that are happening in the world find it hard to tell what to grab and what to let go. People around them keep telling them to let go of old skills and dreams, but they continue carrying them around because they don't realize what they are carrying. To reboot in a new era, you must shake off old practices. Keep only the framework of your life and change everything else, including past methods. Only then can you accept and bring in new thoughts, new roles, and new methods, all of which you need to save your job, money, family, and future. You can be reborn as a competent person only when you change everything.

CHAPTER 9

IN UNCERTAIN TIMES, THINK IN SCENARIOS

Thomas Frey, senior futurist at the DaVinci Institute and Google's top-rated futurist speaker, wrote that the effect of coronavirus is like "hitting a giant reset button for planet earth."[26]

This "reset button" is often associated with rebooting a computer, and the term "reboot" is often used in the movie industry as well. There, reboots occur when filmmakers take the characters, plot, and backstory with which a movie started and change them all to make a completely different film.

Leading scholars define post-coronavirus as a "grand tran-

---

26 Thomas Frey, "19 Startling COVID Trends and 19 Golden COVID Opportunities Emerging from the Chaos," Futurist Speaker, March 20, 2020, https://futuristspeaker.com/futurist-thomas-frey-insights/covid-19-startling-trends-and-19-golden-opportunities-emerging-from-the-chaos/.

sitional time," where everything stops and everything changes. You cannot catch up in this time by making small changes. As Batman rebooted with *Batman Begins*, we have no choice but to lay down all the existing things and reboot. The best thing that you can do at the moment is reboot: turn it all off and turn it on again. Fortunately, or unfortunately, the only thing left for us, whose lives automatically came to a pause due to the coronavirus, is to restart the engine.

There is one condition for restarting life. The main character remains the same, but the scenario must be written differently. In my case, the only thing that I kept was the most basic element: my career as a motivational speaker. I changed all the rest–the speaking style that I'd been stubbornly insisting on using, my know-how, and the platform by which I reached my audiences. Creating a scenario in which all these elements have changed is what is saving me in the post-coronavirus period. If you are determined to resurface as a competent person in the new world, you have to write your own "reboot scenario" every day.

WRITE A LIFE SCENARIO IN THE FACE OF UNCERTAINTY

"What should I do, MK?"

This is the most common question I've been asked since the coronavirus outbreak began. From a small business owner who was hit by the coronavirus pandemic just a week after opening his business to a single mom, who after working at home for two weeks, received a text message notifying her that she had been laid off to a Korean-American who had leased a house in London to start an Airbnb but hadn't had a single guest for several months.

No one was prepared for this, so no one knows how to move forward. Even though we're all dealing with the same situation, it's affecting each of us differently, and each of our solutions will be unique. Listening to the stories of people who were struggling, including my own daughter and brother, I wanted to give them at least some straws to grasp at, but it was difficult to give them any answers because I was not directly involved in their situations. While racking my brain to figure out how we could all pull through this crisis together, I came up with the idea of asking them to start writing their own scenarios. I wanted to tell them to join hands with me and urgently search together for a solution to save ourselves in the midst of chaos.

While reading various references and reports about the post-coronavirus world, I was most intrigued by those released by global consulting firms such as McKinsey & Company, Bain & Company, and the Boston Consulting Group. Scenario development was the main focus of all their reports. Each was packed with all kinds of scenarios, including one that analyzed various timeline models to predict when the pandemic would come to an end, a scenario that showed the global economic downturn curve, and a scenario that predicted economic impacts by industry.

People often think of movies or plays when talking about imagined scenarios, but in the business world, scenario management is used to inform and prepare strategies, which take into consideration a number of variables, to cope with uncertain economic conditions. Therefore, scenarios commonly refer to future forecast reports that contain countermeasures that are appropriate for various situations that may arise in the future. So is the scenario only necessary for large economic units, such as countries, industries, and corporations?

It is not just countries or the businesses that are facing uncertainty due to the coronavirus. The economic recession is threatening the livelihoods of individuals and of many self-employed and small-business owners who have been forced to close their businesses because of the social distancing policy. I've met many small- and large-business owners, but only a very few of them have told me that they were having a coronavirus-induced business boom. When companies struggle, it naturally affects the domestic economy in turn.

What's more, uncertainty is growing even worse. Nobody can tell if the economy will get better or worse in the aftermath of coronavirus, how long the pandemic will last, and when the economy will start to rebound. If scenario modeling is necessary in order to deal with an uncertain future, perhaps individuals like us need scenarios more than countries and corporations do.

AN EXERCISE IN MAKING YOUR DREAMS COME TRUE

We are living in a time when drafting your life scenario is a necessity. To respond sensitively to unpredictable changes, we must look ahead, take action, and whenever necessary, modify our plans. And we must keep repeating this process over and over again.

That is why I think that a "reboot scenario" is what we, as individuals, need most. Companies rich with resources are spending a lot of money to bring brains together at their affiliated economic or strategic research institutes to write scenarios and put together action strategies. But what about individuals who don't have access to the collective brainpower of experts? They must mobilize all their time and resources to write their own scenarios. To be brutally honest, there is nobody who genuinely cares about you except yourself. When hit by a crisis, you are on your own to confront and overcome the problem.

What you need to write is a reboot scenario that will save

your life. A scenario is a workbook, where you practice how to make your dreams come true. That's what you've been doing all your life; you just need to write down what you need to do and use that scenario to reach your goals.

Let me briefly introduce you to the three stages of writing a reboot scenario—a process that I've been following and modifying repeatedly for the past several months.

The first stage in writing a reboot scenario is analyzing the changes happening to you and the world post-coronavirus. Imagine that the world is your stage, and you have often been the leading character in plays. You are still playing the leading role, but this time, the stage has changed. To continue to be the leading character, you must carry yourself differently, walking confidently onto the new stage. To do this, you will have to look at the stage setting and note what has changed, what has remained the same, and what you need to keep as is, add to, or dispose of entirely.

The second step involves writing a brief synopsis of your scenario by applying four Reboot Formulas to your dreams. If a scenario refers to a full-length script, a synopsis is a summary of its plot line. You may need to consider a few different factors or pathways to the successful scenario. With strong analysis and constant creative brainstorming about how things might be different in the wake of the coronavirus, you can create the right scenario for yourself. If you're worried about finding the right scenario, just start writing. Start with a ten-line synopsis about the future you want. As long as you keep writing, specific solutions will gradually start to reveal themselves.

The final stage is to map out a to-do list of all the tasks that you'll need to complete in order to achieve your new scenario. The best, most useful scenario will result from specific lists. You need to plan concrete actions to take in order to ensure that you're moving in the right direction.

A scenario is not a fixed work schedule: it is a dynamically changing design. Instead of following a scenario that someone else has written for you, you, as the main character, write and rewrite your scenario every day to ensure that you fit into the changing world. While writing a scenario that is only for you, you will learn how to reboot yourself into a competent person.

CHAPTER 10

HOW TO WRITE YOUR OWN REBOOT SCENARIO

STAGE 1. ANALYZE YOURSELF AND THE WORLD

Ji-yoon is an editor working for a publishing company, and one day she came to see me in my office with a question.

I was seriously thinking about starting my own company when, suddenly, the coronavirus happened. I didn't think it was a good idea to quit my job at this point–at least not for a while–but it's also hard to give up my dream. What do you think I should do?

Having been an editor at the publishing company for fourteen years, she has extensive connections, a broad range of interests, and the ability to bring together the right people.

In fact, Ji-yoon started thinking about becoming an independent business owner several years ago. The widespread usage of smartphones changed the way people consumed media, and the company's book sales declined year over year no matter how hard they tried to promote and sell them. The company eventually started putting pressure on employees to publish more books in order to maintain sales, which resulted in less time being given to publish each book. Publishing became a chore, rather than the fun career it has been when she started. She was afraid that she was no longer contributing to the publishing of quality books. That's when she started thinking hard about how she could publish quality books that would satisfy both readers and herself. It seems to me that Ji-yoon was right to be concerned about her job situation, particularly because I've heard from numerous people that the publishing industry is continuing to decline, and the market is growing smaller due to the limited number of Korean-speaking readers.

"I think you should be careful about quitting your job at this moment. But I know you are not the kind who can easily give up your dream."

"Right. Honestly, I haven't had enough time to think ahead to what I would do and how I could become independent because I've been living in the present all these years. So I thought I should just consider that coronavirus is giving me some extra time to think more about it. But I don't know where and how to start. I've been working on salary all my life and becoming an independent business owner is really easier said than done. Do you even think that's possible?"

"Actually, you came to me at just the right time. Recently, I've been writing my life reboot scenario, and I wonder if it could be of help to you. Would you give it a try?"

"What do I do? I'd love to give it a try!"

Ji-yoon and I decided to meet every weekend and write our own life scenarios. The first stage starts by analyzing yourself and the world.

WHAT ARE MY CORE COMPETENCIES THAT ARE STILL IN DEMAND?

The objective of writing a life scenario is to make visible your plan for living in a changed world. The first thing you need to know is yourself–the main character of the scenario. There are many tools that you can use to analyze yourself, but there are two things to focus on: one is to identify which of your skills and plans for the future you should keep, and the other is to determine what you should improve on.

I asked Ji-yoon to write down which of her current job skills she thought might still be in demand in the post-coronavirus world. She thought hard for a while before she came up with a few skills.

> I think I'm good at communicating with my writers. When a preliminary table of contents is submitted, most editors wait until the deadline, when the author submits the completed manuscript, but I give feedback to authors each time they submit a part of the manuscript. When I have time, I contact them by phone or visit them in person. Whatever they need, I do everything possible to get it for them, and if they hit a bump, I work together with them to get past it. People around me tell me that I am already busy enough and I should stop wasting time doing these things, but I think it has been a tremendous help to me because by doing these things, I have learned how to make the most out of the authors' abilities, communicate with them, and solve problems quickly.

If you ask me, Ji-yoon's real competitive edge is her perseverance. She works so hard, both on weekdays and weekends, that she is in a category of her own–driven even more than the average workaholic. No matter how exhausted she is, she immediately perks up when somebody mentions something about her work. I myself am confident in my determination, but Ji-yoon is as determined as I am, if not more so.

Ultimately, moving into a world with so many unknowns, you must decide what would be your safest bet for the future.

Taking inventory of what you know, what people value, and what you need to improve is critical for ensuring your success when the pandemic is over.

Jenny is the managing director of our company headquarters. She is slow in almost every way, but when it comes to digital technology, she learns everything faster than anyone else. She taught herself and mastered YouTube to an expert level in a month, and now she is learning with me how to code. I can tell that she understands coding better than most people. If there is a task that makes young employees struggle, she can get it done in just a few days, once she applies himself. But it seems that she is not aware of how good she is at it. One day, I told her how impressive her speed is when it comes to learning digital technology. She didn't accept the compliment instantly; she couldn't see it herself. Sometimes people around you know you better than you know yourself.

In order to get the most accurate analysis of your core competencies, you may have to show your notes to trusted friends and colleagues. Ask them for their feedback–if there's anything you missed or might have gotten wrong about yourself. It's important to get objective opinions so that your future will be as successful as possible.

IDENTIFY SKILLS THAT NEED TO BE UPDATED FOR THE FUTURE

To be a competent person in a changed world, you will have to update and improve on some of your skills. Knowing what core competencies you already have is important, but knowing what you need to update and work on to become more competent is just as important. Supposing the core competencies you have now are constants, the final answers about your perfect future scenario can come out completely differently depending on who works on what and how fast and properly.

When I asked Ji-yoon to write down what she needed to improve, she quickly wrote down what she needed to work on to develop her skills.

These days, it's important to promote business on social media. So I think I should study platform marketing. I also need to quickly grasp the latest trends of the publishing industry because the publishing market will go through a significant change in post-coronavirus. I should have a good understanding of publishing trends overseas because I should proactively export books to overseas markets beyond the limited market for Korean-speaking readers. That means, I need to study English, and I should also learn bookkeeping because I need to become capable of managing the finances if I'm going independent.

There's nothing difficult about it. You just need to write

down the things that you are not good at or the things that you always thought you should learn about. There are no wrong answers, and nobody is there to grade you. And because you wrote them down doesn't mean you must follow through on them. Just write down what comes to your mind, and remember, the more, the better.

DECIDE WHAT WILL CHANGE AND WHAT WILL REMAIN IN YOUR INDUSTRY

When you have finished analyzing yourself, it is time to analyze the world in which you'll live. Admittedly, this is the hard part. When it comes to analyzing yourself, the answers come easily because you know what and who you are. But when it comes to the world, there are more things you don't know about than you know. I reached out and asked Choi Yun-sik, director of the Institute for Human Resources in Asia and the author of numerous books on predictions for the future, such as *Five Years from Now: A U.S.-China War Scenario* and *Five Years from Now: The Future of Korea Scenario*. Wondering how the futurist author was analyzing the world, I asked him for a meeting, with high expectations. However, his answer to my question was rather simple.

He said, "Just because I am a futurist doesn't mean I can write with extraordinary skill. At first, I roughly write down what I think would change and what I think would remain the same. I just write down whatever comes to mind and that's how I begin my prediction of the future. Then I add findings from my studies and research before I have a report on predicting the future as we know it."

Listening to him, I thought that this was something that I could absolutely do myself. I thought I should write down what I thought would change in the world and what would remain the same, all from my own perspective. In my case, people's desire to listen to motivational speeches will remain the same, but their access to those speeches will be completely different. What about Ji-yoon's publishing industry?

I think that the desire for paper books and other written materials will remain the same in the future. Of course, there is a growing demand for videos, but they won't completely replace hard-copy texts. Instead, people will use hard-copy materials in many ways. Have you ever heard of a chatbook? The genre is becoming popular these days, and it refers to an e-book that's written in dialogue, as if characters are chatting. I think that many diverse forms of books will be introduced in the future.

It is difficult to identify the things that will remain the same in the future. The only thing that we can be sure of is that no matter how much the world changes, well-made products will always sell. The only thing that I or anyone else will be able to control is how well we do the thing we're best at. So I decided to accept the fact that everything was going to change except my own core competencies. I felt so much lighter and more focused the moment that I accepted that reality.

In order to craft an actionable Reboot Scenario, we still have to identify what will change. Ask yourself: What are the things that are obviously changing right now? You won't find the answer just by contemplation; you must search for it. Actively seek new information and identify trends. In my search, I learned that there was no better resource than the latest news reports. First, I opened the internet search engines, entered my job, and read articles that I got as search results. I also entered queries as simple as "the things that coronavirus is changing," and I read news articles that I got as search results. This might not sound very impressive, but nothing was more helpful than news reports for finding out what was changing in my industry. Ji-yoon told me, "My company's PR team compiles articles about the publishing industry and sends them to me. So I thought that I was well informed about the latest trends in the publishing industry. After hearing what you said, I searched for articles and found a lot of new information that I hadn't known. I guess that I should look up news articles more frequently."

You are the only person who can identify the changes taking place in your industry that are relevant to you. Even looking at the same piece of information, some people might find it just a random story about what's going on in the world, while others might believe that it is an extremely important piece of information. You can get more diverse insights from the information you find yourself than from what's been compiled for you by others.

I spent most of this stage searching for information. I analyzed the changes happening around me by reading a wide variety of information sources, such as newspapers, books, and reports. While doing this, I realized that searching for information is a skill in itself. The more you do it, the more skilled you become and the more capable you are of finding more premium information. At first, you might be a little sloppy, but if you keep at it, you will soon become well versed with the trends happening in your industry.

As you refine your list of the skills that you need to keep and improve and of what will change and what will remain the same, you will notice yourself responding to your searches almost subconsciously by drawing lines. You draw lines to connect relevant pieces of information together, and at some point, it creates a chemical reaction. Through this chemical reaction comes a stream of new ideas, such as, "If I learned this digital technology and applied it to my marketing, I would be able to attract more customers" or "Since this is emerging as a promising new industry, I would definitely become competitive if I started preparing for it now."

I know a CEO of a startup who is in his late twenties and

has a new business idea each time I see him. He must have shared at least fifty with me in the time we've known each other. Now his train of ideas is running at an accelerated speed because his existing and newly acquired competencies are in sync with the changes that have been happening in the world lately. I imagine that even at this moment, he is drawing numerous lines in his brain.

If you have finished writing down your list and you still don't feel a spark of excitement, it means that your analysis is incomplete. Don't be discouraged: you simply need to keep studying, keep looking for those dots to connect. Continue to ask those around you, lean on experts in your industry, and refine your lists daily. One day soon, it will all make sense, and you'll know exactly what to do in the post-coronavirus world.

STAGE 2. WRITE A TEN-LINE SYNOPSIS BY APPLYING THE REBOOT FORMULAS

USE YOUR IMAGINATION TO WRITE A TEN-LINE SYNOPSIS

Last year, I posted "MK's Ten-Line Diary" on Instagram. At first, I started writing ten-line diary entries whenever I made a resolution or had a new idea so that I would not forget them. Gradually, the activity turned into a habit similar to keeping a daily journal. Whenever I forgot the resolution I'd made previously, I would read through the ten-line diary entries that I had shared on Instagram, and this refreshed my resolution. For me, the ten-line diary was a guide to pulling my thoughts together, following through on my resolutions, and adding a sense of anticipation to my daily life.

When the coronavirus crisis hit and all routines went out the window, I started writing things down again. Every time I found a small clue to pulling through the crisis, I wrote it down in my notebook, as I did in the ten-line diary. At first, I wrote these down rather casually, but after I learned how to write a scenario, I started grouping them into what I needed to keep, what I needed to improve, what is likely to change, and what is likely to remain the same—all based on my own criteria. When all the small clues were put together, they created new combinations and provided me with solutions one by one. Just a few days ago, my ten-line entry read:

> If we are to survive in this changed world, we must transform our company into a content-providing IT company. For this to happen, I, the president of the company, must be the first to study digital technology. I must also hire IT specialists. Together with them, I will have to carry out the research needed to decide what kind of technology we need to adopt in our content products in order to create the best synergy. We also have to upgrade our systems and content every day. The online college, MKYU, must also be revamped. Wouldn't it be a great help if whenever neces-

sary MKYU offered classes for digitally illiterate students? I must take preparatory steps right now to put together such an education system as soon as possible.

This determined, resolute ten-line statement is my own manifesto, which I have declared in response to the changed world. Countless people all over the world have been making their own manifestos since the outbreak of coronavirus. Companies are unveiling new businesses every day, and governments are also introducing new policies–all in an effort to respond to the new world. These responses will eventually change the world that we live in. Given that eventuality, don't we all need to declare our own ten-line manifestos in response to the changes happening in the world? In terms of our scenarios, these manifestos will be equivalent of the synopses that summarize the key plot.

In Stage 1, we have identified what we need to keep and improve, as well as what is likely to change and what is likely remain the same. In Stage 2, we use those findings to write a ten-line synopsis. It is our way of declaring to the changing world what we will do to confront it and win.

When I asked Ji-yoon to write her ten-line synopsis, she wrote:

Even in a changed world, paper books will survive. I would like to distribute quality books to more readers in the wider world and enjoy a greater sense of reward. K-books can join the parade of the Korean wave that is marching around the world and stand side by side with K-pops and K-dramas. At a time when Korea is grabbing the attention of the world with its successful control of the spread of coronavirus, I want to take this as an opportunity to become someone who distributes Korean-made quality content products to the entire world. To make this happen, I should improve my foreign language and digital skills.

One of the misguided ideas that people have is that inspiration comes suddenly, like a flash of lightning. That's not true. Inspiration happens when you see something unfamiliar, come upon new information, meet someone who works in a different field, or become aware of something that you've never paid attention to before. A clash with something unfamiliar creates a crack in your existing ideas, and out of that crack sprouts a new idea.

That's what happened to Ji-yoon. She had already written her synopsis, but when she read an article about Bill Gates that said he had commended Korea's measures against the spread of coronavirus and had contributed a large sum of money to a Korean company, she came up with the idea of K-book that might take over the world like K-pop and K-drama. Some might say that the idea is ridiculous. They might shake their heads, pointing out that there have been many similar attempts, but none of them has succeeded. Yet, all those numerous inventions that changed human civilization started with someone's crazy imagination!

To be honest, when my employees were talking about webtoons, I thought that they should spend their time reading books instead. I couldn't figure out why they were so focused on childish cartoons. But my idea about webtoons was shattered when I saw an article about a cartoonist who presented a controversial claim. It was then proven by a researcher, and defined by a scientist. I learned that cartoons are one step ahead of our time.

The ingenuity that breaks through the boundary of impossibility without being restricted to complicated theories and calculation and the daring courage that expands the range of human thoughts beyond space into another world, as in sci-fi movies—that's the kind of imagination that we find in webtoons. It is also the kind of imagination that we must have now, when we are living in a time when we cannot predict what will happen next week or next month.

When imagining something new, it is also necessary to let your brain go as wild as it can. It's okay to be outrageous. Let the imagination go as far as it wants, even if it pops like a bubble in the next stage. If you fear failure, even in your imagination, you cannot start anything.

A good synopsis is the kind that gets people to say, "No way!"

But if your friend tells you, "I think it's a good idea; give it a try," then chances are, your synopsis is not strong enough. At a time when everything is changing by the hour and the minute, an outrageous vision of your future may have a higher probability of actually happening than a more tame, "reasonable" one.

PERFECT YOUR SYNOPSIS BY APPLYING THE REBOOT FORMULAS

When you have finished writing a ten-line synopsis, it's time for one of the most important steps. You must review this synopsis in light of the four post-coronavirus Reboot Formulas: on-tact, digital transformation, independent worker, and safety. You may have the greatest plan ever, but if it fails to fit into the new world, it is nothing but a pie-in-the-sky dream. The synopsis is only an outcome of your imagination, and if you want to bring it to life and become your solution, you must clear it through the four Reboot Formulas.

In the case of Ji-yoon, she sent me another synopsis just a few days later. It was about the business model she was thinking of using when she starts her own business, and she wanted me to review it and see if it met the requirements of the four Reboot Formulas.

Ji-yoon's new synopsis read:

In the near future, I will be running a publishing agency that sells to domestic and overseas publishers the rights to manuscripts written by Korean authors. Competent writers will receive support from this agency at every step of the way, from coming up with an idea to actually writing the manuscript. My main duty will be to communicate with domestic and foreign publishers and sell to them the publishing rights of those manuscripts. I will get added value when publishers compete with one another for the rights to sell in their respective language, allowing me to get the highest possible offers. While writers are completing their manuscripts, they will be told at what price their manuscripts were sold. I will expand the publishing market for K-books by expanding into K-pop and K-drama.

Of course, I could have racked my brain to find solutions for her, but I don't know anything about the publishing industry. Besides, I have always believed that when it comes to your own problems, you only get useful answer when you solve those problems yourself. So the next day, I called Ji-yoon into my office, and together we reviewed her synopsis, running it through the four formulas. I asked questions and she answered them.

"What do you think the answer would be if you applied the 'on-tact' formula to your publishing agency business model?" I asked.

She answered, "Well, it will be difficult, but I think it will be possible if I add digital communication tools to it."

"Have you thought about how?" I challenged her.

Ji-yoon responded, "A publishing agency's ability to compete depends on how good its content is. To appeal to potential buyers without meeting them, I should create an open platform, where I can disclose which project I am working on, with which writer, and where people can get access to the platform by signing up for a subscription service."

"Yes, that sounds good. Have you ever thought about the digital transformation formula?" I asked.

"No. That was the hardest part. I'm good at producing paper books, but I don't have much experience with digital," she said.

The managing director of our company, Jenny, was quietly listening to our conversation, and at this point, she joined our conversation and said, "I read a report about a publishing company in Britain, and according to the report, this company is releasing one bestseller after another. It turns out that this company has a website where aspiring writers are free to post any of their writings, and the company analyzes readers' response to them. Based on these responses, the company picks the ones that are most likely to become the next bestsellers. I checked out their website to see how it worked, and I thought that we could easily follow the same model. If we just run a big data-crawling program, we can have the same system in just a day. What if we used this approach as a benchmark?"

Jenny and I could understand how it worked because at that time we were learning Python from a big data expert, but to Ji-yoon it probably sounded like Greek. That's how I felt in the beginning.

However, Ji-yoon asked a few questions and quickly comprehended what Jenny was talking about. She said, "So it's like using the information you collect from readers' social media to create big data, which helps you find the keywords that are trending in the publishing industry, isn't it? I see how you can collect accurate information faster by running the program than by relying on an editor. And I can tell that the findings would be relayed to writers to assist them in developing their work. It sounds like a great idea."

To pass your scenario through the digital filter, it is critical that you yourself understand digital technology. You don't necessarily have to learn it, but just knowing what kinds of digital technology are out there and available can enable you to come up with ideas and figure out how to apply them in your business. The more your business belongs to traditional industry groups, the more it is critical to study digital technology.

I asked Ji-yoon, "If you start your own business, you literally become an independent worker. What do you think you will need most when that happens?"

She said:

> Getting investors would be the key to success, don't you think? I have a few people around me who have expressed interest in my business, but you never know what will actually happen. I think that it might help if I studied the startup ecosystem and also made personal connections with venture capitalists. And I think that I need collaboration tools or messenger tools to ensure smooth communication with publishers and publishing agencies overseas. I should start learning how to use the collaboration tools that are most widely used in other countries.

Going forward, it will be difficult to make your business appeal to customers unless your product or service can make it past the safety filter. I've met numerous editors working for many publishing companies, but never have I seen an editor as smart as Ji-yoon. Nevertheless, there is a subject with which even a smart editor like her must struggle to come to terms: safety.

This time, I gave her a tip by telling her:

While writing a book, I did a lot of research into climate change. Everything that I read was informational and useful, but the only problem was that most references were written in language that was much too technical. Try to come up with books that will make people feel that they can relate to the subject. It doesn't necessarily have to be any of the conventional genres. It could be a novel, essay, and even a comic. What do you think?

She said, "When it comes to developing book ideas, I can start right away. I will remember that safety should be an important element."

It is harder than you think to create a ten-line synopsis that will pass the test of the Reboot Formulas. I wrote about them rather simply in this book, but the truth is that it took me several days to reach a conclusion that would help Ji-yoon. She felt as though she had completed a big assignment, but she will find herself taking on bigger assignments with every answer she uncovers. While scrambling to apply the four Reboot Formulas in business, some people seize the opportunity of a lifetime, while others are completely devastated. But there is nothing to worry about.

Creating a synopsis is not a homework assignment that is completed when you have written it down. You can write a new synopsis each time you come up with a new idea, and you can modify your synopsis every time you come across something new. You can change, rewrite, or even delete your synopsis at any time. What matters is that the more you apply yourself to writing a synopsis, the more it becomes part of your routine. The more you refine your thoughts, the more solutions you will find. It is important to just start writing down whatever comes to mind instead of trying to create something perfect from the very beginning. Just keep imagining and applying the formulas to what you write, and when you repeatedly practice this process, you will eventually have a lifesaving scenario that you have never imagined possible.

STAGE 3. CREATE AND EXECUTE TO-DO LISTS IMMEDIATELY

Once you have created your own synopsis using a webtoon-caliber, wild imagination and have filtered it through the four formulas, it is time to move on to Stage 4: creating to-do lists to bring your reboot scenario to life.

In the case of Ji-yoon, her list includes the expansion of a network in the domestic publishing industry, making connections with overseas publishers, and studying English and digital technology, all of which are necessary to build an open platform that reflects the latest trends in Korean books. But she needs to get more granular than that to stay on track. She needs to outline each subtask for the most important to-dos on her list.

Making all these lists is not the end of it. What is important is their execution; taking action is essential to making the most out of them. To ensure that you complete all the necessary actions, persevering no matter how many problems you encounter, be sure to keep in mind the level of difficulty of each task and the time you will need to accomplish it. Space them out accordingly so that you maintain a positive trajectory and remain focused. No matter how good a plan is, it's useless if you cannot execute it.

You can maximize results by executing your plans with a team instead of working alone. There is a good possibility that there are people who have knowledge of most of the specifics that you never knew about. You can cut down the time that you have to spend studying the issues if you meet people who work in relevant industries and ask for their help instead of trying to do everything alone.

You must also keep modifying your scenario by incorporating into it the lessons that you have learned from your failures. If luck is with you, you will hit the jackpot with the first scenario that you have created, but if not, you might end up wasting time and effort. From my lengthy experience, no action is wasted entirely. Even if it results in the worst outcome, you can learn a lesson from it and avoid making wrong choices the next time.

As I said earlier, I write my reboot scenarios in my workbook, where I figured out how to make my dreams come true despite the coronavirus outbreak. I write in this workbook every day. When I say that I am writing a scenario, you might get the impression that I am writing some grand story, but the truth is that my scenario is just a scribble in a workbook, where I write down questions such as, "What changes will be happening post-coronavirus?" "What do I need to start doing to survive?" "What kind of a motivational speaker should I be from now on?" "How will I be making a living in the future?" "What kind of a person should I be in the future?" In hard times such as those that we are going through now, you need to practice using a workbook, and you should not jump into it without any preparation. You must repeatedly go through the process of imagining yourself in the future, write to-do lists, take action, and modify your scenario.

After reading the scenarios of companies and global consulting firms, it suddenly dawned on me that their scenarios most likely will change in the future. After studying and predicting the future, putting together strategies, and taking action on each, while continuously modifying their scenarios, they might see the moment when their present meets the future someday. The content of their scenarios is not what is important; what is important is their commitment to repeatedly rewriting and executing them.

An individual's reboot scenario does not contain only predictions. It also contains the person's commitment to following through. Once the third stage of writing a scenario and the execution of the action plan become a habit, we as individuals can also see the moment when the present meets the future. No future is created just by imagination. You can perfect your lifesaving scenario only by going through a series of failures and constant modifications. When you attempt something that you've never done before, failure gives you a way to judge the soundness of your scenario. Once you begin to execute it, you can tell instantly if your plan is good or bad. The result of your execution can be either a failure or a success, but whichever it is, looking back at it can be the best way to identify what you need to modify in your next scenario.

In 2013, when I wrote the book *MK Kim's Dream On*, I said that a dream must be born out of deprivation. Now we must make a move not because we are deprived but because we are desperate. We might not have as much time as we think. We must sit down and start writing a scenario immediately. Our imagination must be as wild as the post-coronavirus world, as we utilize the four Reboot Formulas to identify the things we need to keep and add to, as well as those that are likely to change and those that are likely to remain the same. We must make specific to-do lists, act immediately, and keep moving forward, one step at a time, while continuously modifying our strategies. By repeating this process infinitely, we will come to discover the "best way to reboot ourselves post-coronavirus."

CHAPTER 11

REBOOTING POWER COMES FROM CHASING

Not long ago, I started an event titled "English Challenge with MK Kim" on Instagram. It was a five-week challenge in which my followers were asked to split the seven-and-a-half-minute TED speech of Angela Lee Duckworth, the author of *Grit*, into smaller clips. They were then to listen to the clips repeatedly for five weeks, until they had memorized the entire speech by heart. When I invited my Instagram followers to take the challenge, nearly 1,000 followers signed up for it.

About two weeks passed after we started the challenge, a few comments left by my followers caught my attention.

"I just found out about this English challenge. Is it too late for me to join? Is it possible for me to start now?"

"I wanted to sign up for it when it first started, but I didn't because I was too lazy. Now it's almost halfway into the challenge, and I guess it's too late to join."

The most common fear of most people was being behind others. It was just two weeks late, or one month for some latecomers, and I couldn't understand why they were so concerned about being late. I thought hard about this for a long time. I wanted to be useful and motivational for all these people who felt concerned that they were behind. I kept coming back to the word "chase." I wanted to tell them about chasing.

I wrote, "Let me tell you a technique that will help you realize your dreams. Tell yourself that it's never too late, take the first step, and start 'chasing.' Of course, sometimes you feel nervous and anxious. That's how I felt when I started studying English when I was over fifty-five. The fastest shortcut to win a challenge is to start chasing it right now."

The rebooting power comes from full-speed chasing. I picked the word "chase" because about 99 percent of the people in the world are chasers. I've been a chaser all my life myself. I've never been ahead of others in anything I did. It was the same in my career as a motivational speaker. When I started making speeches in company settings in the 1990s, there were already numerous motivational speakers. There were speakers specializing in every subject–time management, workplace etiquette, image making, leadership, and communication–and they had already cemented their reputations in the industry. I always started one step behind others; I always had to chase those who were running ahead of me. I have had to chase one goal after another, be it succeeding in my career as a motivational speaker or as a YouTube creator.

Why do people think it's too late if they haven't started from the same place as others? Why do they feel defeated before they even start? Why can't they define the day that they make a resolution and start working on it as their own "day one"? Comparing your day one to that of others only makes beginning that much harder.

You should never hesitate or feel defeated at the starting line just because you came later than others. It is normal to start as a chaser when there are already millions of dots laid out before you. Don't push yourself to be the first dot or one of the first ten out of several millions. That doesn't happen in life.

If you want to reboot, you must become a hell-bent chaser.

THREE SECRETS TO BECOMING A CHASER
START AS FAST AS YOU CAN

The key to chasing is speed. If you start your chase but don't complete it swiftly, it's pointless. Too many people let themselves run in idle before they start moving, only to stop too soon. To succeed in an unknown future, you must operate at top speed from the beginning. And don't let up until you're finished.

The secret to speeding up from day one of your chasing is to set goals for yourself. You can't simply say that you are ready to learn English; you have to take the first step. Buy a book, download an app, or search online videos that can help you move toward that goal. As you see yourself succeeding, you'll be more determined to keep your winning streak going.

Proof of our accomplishments is empowering. Stack up as much proof as possible from the very beginning, and you'll be more inclined to keep pushing, full speed ahead.

BE CONFIDENT

For a chaser, confidence is a must-have fuel. Without confidence, you are bound to slow down and eventually come to a stop. In an intense situation, you need to keep running, but you cannot maintain your speed when you continue to be distracted. Then the question is, how do you forge a conviction that tells you, "After all, it was the right decision"?

Confidence doesn't come from determination; it comes from success. If you want to convince yourself that it was a good idea to study English, you must prove it by taking an English test and getting a good score, traveling to an English-speaking country and experiencing the pleasure of communicating with locals, or getting a job promotion after having your English proficiency recognized. Those proofs instantly bring you confidence and fuel you to continuously chase your dreams.

NEVER GIVE UP

Day One: 875 people. Day Six: 288 people. These are the number of participants who stayed on my Instagram English challenge. Two weeks later, the number went down to just one-third of the initial number. What surprised me was that half of the remaining participants turned out to be real chasers. At the beginning, those who started early stood out, but at the end, the winners proved to be those who had started late. The feeling that they were handicapped by having joined the race later than the others actually spurred them on.

On day six, two-thirds of the way into the challenge, I posted a message on Instagram declaring that it was a new day one. I wanted to refresh the initial determination of those who remained, while telling the latecomers that it was their day one of the challenge. I wanted to tell them not to give up their dreams, that they can start working toward them any-time, and that they should find the energy they needed to increase the speed at which they were chasing those dreams. Thankfully, they responded to my efforts to cheer them up and encourage them by perking up their courage.

"I'm late too, but I'm thinking of today as the day I am beginning, and I will follow through diligently on my commitment."

"The phrase 'day one' really came home to me. I'm in."

"I will never give up my dreams, and I will go all the way to the end. My chasing started belatedly, but I'll finish what I started."

Most of us are ordinary people—not extraordinary people who are out in front in this turbulent world. But just because we are not at the front doesn't mean that we cannot follow the road. I believe that the bravest choice that ordinary people with dreams can make is "to chase." No start is more courageous than chasing. Just take one step forward, even if you are afraid or have no confidence. And speed up. You will find confidence and self-assurance on the way. I believe that we will bring ourselves and our dreams back to life again by taking up this special journey called chasing.

PART 4

YOU MUST BE A NEW LEARNER TO KEEP YOUR WORK

When studying in one area, we need to study in other, related one in order to acquire broad knowledge, across multiple disciplines. The emergence of new products and services will create a phenomenon where new jobs will repeatedly be created and then disappear. Under these circumstances, your survival depends on whether you can learn quickly and apply that knowledge to your job. Therefore, you need to ask yourself: Am I a new learner? Am I ready to become one?

CHAPTER 12

THE ERA OF JUST-IN-TIME EDUCATION IS HERE

Our company will become a content company, while at the same time being a digital company. To make this happen, all employees must be able to communicate and collaborate with IT professionals. Understanding trends and applying them to your work is essential. If you don't study constantly from now on, you won't be able to keep up with the pace at which our company grows.

This is what I declared to all employees just a few days after completing my scenario. I announced to them that we were transforming into a digital company to save the company, while at the same time finding hidden opportunities in the current crisis. I wanted to be clear that just as the luxury brand Burberry went "full digital Burberry," the motivational speaker MK Kim was also going "full digital MK Kim."

As I made my announcement, I saw tension in the faces of my employees. Since all our business lines were going online at the time, they were busy getting used to new work tools and making new business plans, and now I was demanding that they constantly study. They likely felt burdened and overwhelmed. But they didn't seem to think of my announcement as the usual nagging from the boss. If I were to guess why, it was because, while doing their work, they had realized how much reality was going to change in the next six months to a year.

Learning, getting educated, and studying are my creed. I was able to transform myself from being an analog speaker to a YouTube creator simply because I've been studying fiercely. When we started our YouTube channels, none of the employees in our company were YouTube experts. I didn't even know what kind of human resources I needed to hire because I was completely ignorant of the subject. I just took and edited videos with my smartphone and uploaded these crude videos to YouTube. The managing director, Jenny, and another director, Min-Kyung, were there at the time, fumbling through the whole process with me.

Before joining our company, Jenny was a reporter. For almost ten years, her main job duties in the company were editing and fine-tuning my language into speeches and content suitable for broadcasting. Then, two years ago, when we started working with YouTube, her job duties changed completely. Now that our content was being delivered through YouTube, she taught herself how to film videos, develop ideas, write subtitles, and even broadcast live. She trained herself further by learning from YouTube's big data, filming, and thumbnail experts. Thanks to her efforts, she became an expert in every job she needs to do to run our YouTube channel, and now she is the head of our video team of over ten employees. She is even consulting for many YouTube channels.

Min-Kyung is the head of our marketing department, and her case is similar to Jenny's. She was a junior motivational speaker, with ten years of experience developing educational curricula. She was in charge of online advertisements and marketing campaigns for our company. When she first started, she knew very little about marketing, but she taught herself by jumping in and trying to find solutions whenever she was called on. Since we launched an online shopping mall, she has been working as a merchandiser–a job she has never done before.

These two directors of our company share something important in common: They both started learning about these jobs after the age of forty. Even though our company completely revamped our business lines while adding new business ventures, they managed to make it through the entire process and even thrived in their careers. Looking back, it has always been part of their daily routines to study something new and immediately apply what they learn to work the entire ten years and over they'd been with me in the company.

"In post-coronavirus, our company will run three times faster than ever. So I ask you to read books and study whenever you have time. If you miss current trends, you won't be able to understand what I'm saying in the future."

I'm witnessing speed and changes that I have never witnessed before. What saved me and my employees is the just-in-time education philosophy that we adopted. It helped us learn and apply new knowledge at lightning speed. If I come across any information that will help us survive, I study and learn about it within the shortest time possible. Sometimes I don't understand all of what I learn, but I grasp enough to see how it will affect my business and how to make the most out of any change that will be for the good of the company. And I expect my employees to demonstrate the same speed and commitment. It may be hard on them, but from now on, just-in-time education will be the norm in our company.

YOU CANNOT EVEN PRACTICE MEDICINE IF YOU DON'T KNOW ARTIFICIAL INTELLIGENCE

If there is a word that has appeared–almost without exception–in the numerous reports released by organizations trying to understand our new reality, it would be "retrain." Amazon, a company that is going through the fastest changes in the world, announced in July 2019 that it will retrain 100,000 of its employees–one-third of the company's entire US workforce.

Jeff Wilke, CEO of Amazon's worldwide consumer business, stated, "Technology is changing our society, and it's certainly changing work...The training programs could help Amazon workers find jobs in different industries."[27]

It sounds good, but the flip side of this statement indicates that even if you are currently working for the world's leading company, you can lose your job at any time if you don't retrain. In Germany, the government took the initiative of offering a similar training policy to prevent unemployment, demonstrating its commitment to resolving issues such as the loss of jobs that was caused by digital technology. In June 2019, the German Ministry of Federal Labor and Social Affairs explained that "we adopted this strategy to 'prevent' unemployment in advance, instead of offering vocational

---

27 Chip Cutter, "Amazon to Retrain a Third of Its U.S. Workforce," *The Wall Street Journal*, July 11, 2019, https://www.wsj.com/articles/amazon-to-retrain-a-third-of-its-u-s-workforce-11562841120.

training when unemployment is about to happen or after it happens. We must change if we want to continue working in the future. And we have to understand that this is a natural part of life."[28]

This statement indicates that retraining used to done just to enable employees to do the same work but with better skills. But the German government was taking the initiative to use digital training as a measure to prevent the loss of jobs. In other words, if you want to continue to work, you must arm yourself with digital retraining.

I have a tutor who is teaching me computer coding. She is a graduate school student majoring in computer engineering. She once told me, "My cousin is a doctor and he suddenly called me and asked me to teach him coding. He said he might not be able to practice medicine if he doesn't know how to communicate with artificial intelligence because AI doctors are being brought into hospitals."

For a while now, we've been hearing a lot about jobs that will disappear in the future, but we assumed that the transformation wouldn't happen for years. But everything we predicted would happen in the distant future is happening now. In late May 2020, it was reported that Microsoft had

28   Ki-chan Kim, "Germany Is Advancing Digital Education for the Whole Nation...'All Citizens Will Not Worry about Future Jobs,'" JoongAng Ilbo, December 3, 2019, https://news.joins.com/article/23647659 (translated to English from source in Korean).

laid off fifty journalists. Those editorial reporters lost their jobs instantly when artificial intelligence took over the news curation job for browsers.[29] Real estate agents have been an integral part of our daily lives, but even they are at risk of losing their jobs. Once blockchain technology is introduced into the real estate market, people will be able to make direct real estate transactions, without having to pay brokers' fees.

World-renowned scholar Yuval Harari terrified us when he predicted that as artificial intelligence replaces human jobs, we humans may degenerate into a useless class.[30] According to him, robots will surpass our physical abilities, and even our mental abilities will be dwarfed by artificial intelligence. As an alternative, he suggested that the governments should consider regulating the speed of their advances: humans should be given more time to adjust to the impact of technology. His viewpoint is based on how difficult it is for individuals to keep pace with the massive changes being brought about by the fourth industrial revolution.

In the end, there is one message that all these changes are giving to us: if we don't learn the latest technology and adapt ourselves to it, we will have no place in the workplace and

---

29 Jim Waterson, "Microsoft Sacks Journalists to Replace Them with Robots," *The Guardian*, May 30, 2020, https://www.theguardian.com/technology/2020/may/30/microsoft-sacks-journalists-to-replace-them-with-robots.

30 Yuval Harari, Speech at World Economic Forum Annual Meeting, accessed February 11, 2021, https://www.weforum.org/agenda/2020/01/yuval-hararis-warning-davos-speech-future-predications/.

will degenerate into a useless class. Training is now a matter of our own survival as well as a part of our daily lives.

In the past, people could keep their jobs and support themselves for twenty to thirty years using only the skills they had learned in their four years of college. That's not today's reality. A college or graduate school degree decreases in value year after year. Education experts predict that in the future, all schools, including universities, will no longer be teaching but learning institutions. According to them, when schools lose their function as teaching institutions, they only need to coach students how to learn on their own. The changes are happening so fast that by the time they graduate from one school, the world will already be so far advanced that what they learned in that school with be obsolete. Quick-thinking young people are already turning their eyes to global online colleges. They already have access to numerous videos of experts in each field, and the best lectures from scholars are available on YouTube. As futurists point out, markets where experts and consumers interact directly with each other are fast approaching.

In addition, as the marriage between the education industry and digital technology gives birth to the edu-tech industry, just-in-time education is growing popular among people who need to learn only what they need and to learn it quickly. The result will be an era of new learners, with access to educational training that will allow them to learn the newly required skills and apply them to their work immediately.

Therefore, we need to reboot our educational methods. We should no longer be studying just to earn a master's or doctorate in one subject; we should be studying a variety of subjects that provide us with an education that will provide us with broad, cross-discipline knowledge. We have seen new jobs emerging and old ones disappearing over the decades, but now that cycle is in years or even months. Under these circumstances, your survival depends on whether you can gain knowledge and quickly apply it to your work.

If you've decided to become a new learner, you need to take responsibility for your own curriculum. No one is going to tell you exactly what to study or how to connect the dots. That's up to you. All individuals who work at different jobs, in different industries must create a personalized curriculum by identifying the knowledge or skills that they urgently need to learn right now and finding out where they can learn them. The first step that new learners must take is identifying exactly which skills they need right now.

In life, we encounter many inflection points, where the directions of our lives change. Just-in-time education is the only way that can ensure that what follows is a rising curve, not a falling one. Once you become a new learner and pass this inflection point, you will find yourself riding on a rising curve before you know it.

CHAPTER 13

SQUARE ONE IS THE BEST PLACE TO START LEARNING

Among the devoted fans of MKTV are many women who are planning their dreams while taking care of their families. Some of the most frequent visitors to my channel are smart women who must stay at home but intend to start working whenever the opportunity arises. In the past, spending time at home instead of working was often detrimental to a woman's career. Women who wanted to reenter the workforce had to go back to square one. Companies often hesitated to hire them back, even if five years before they had been in high-level positions, where they had demonstrated great competence. In those five years, the workplace had changed completely, as the tools and solutions needed to do your job have shifted. To be successful in marketing, for example, you can no longer rely only on traditional marketing skills; you need to be able to analyze, in real time, the digital and big data that you collect from social media. In just two years from now, a number of IT technologies may converge with marketing, making you a stranger even to the marketing terms that will be in use then. At a time when everyone else is using 5G communication and you are still using an antiquated flip phone, you will feel like an "old-timer."

But there's another way to think about this situation. Starting from zero means that you have complete freedom to create the right path for yourself. It doesn't happen only to women whose career track has been interrupted; anybody can suddenly find themselves back at square one, as we stand at the cusp of the fourth industrial revolution. There is no exception to this–even if you have a degree from a prestigious college, work for a large corporation, are a professional such as a doctor or lawyer, or like me, someone who all my life has been making a living by speaking. What you learned three years ago can be just as useless as what you learned five years ago.

If everybody is reset at zero, you can change the game starting now. You can be successful by turning yourself into a new learner and a fierce chaser. If you are a woman whose career track has been interrupted, you have the advantage of being able to manage your time with more flexibility than working women. If you can make the most out of your time and fully apply yourself to learning new skills and knowledge, you can grow into an expert in your field faster than your counterparts.

So what you need to start right now is just-in-time education: studying what you need to learn in order to be able to do work you want and not to have your career track interrupted again. As certain knowledge or skills can broaden your options and they are within your reach, find a way to learn them. Even thinking about doing this might be intimidating, but it can be done if you start at the elementary level.

STEP 1. FAMILIARIZE YOURSELF WITH DIGITAL PLATFORMS AND SERVICES

The easiest way to familiarize yourself with digital platforms, especially if, like most of us, you're starting at square one, is to use digital services that have already been developed into products and observe how they work. The latest Samsung smartphones have built-in, blockchain-based apps called dApps and blockchain wallet.[31] Use these apps and experience how cryptocurrencies are traded and how the blockchain technology is used in real life. Blockchain real estate services that allow you to invest in buildings with as little as $5 have already been launched in Korea.

---

31 Eun-jin Kim, "Samsung to Build Blockchain Ecosystem ahead of Google and Apple," Business Korea, November 5, 2019, http://www.businesskorea.co.kr/news/articleView. html?idxno=37647.

If you are self-employed or a freelancer, you can use a video-editing app to edit videos that you have taken with your smartphone and upload them onto YouTube. You can also make product-promoting posters, with various promotional-image-poster-creating apps and post them on Instagram. It is also recommended that you look for keywords that are trending on Google and use them to run ads on Instagram or Facebook. During this process, you will learn how to achieve the best results on social media, while advertising at a low cost.

The important thing is to practice everything that you do in your daily life on digital. When digital becomes as familiar and natural to you as breathing, the gap between users and producers gradually narrows. While shopping on a mobile device, you find that some apps make it easy for you to navigate and pay, while others are so inconvenient to use that you delete them right away. While observing which Instagram ads make you click on to watch and which you skip, your knowledge as a professional user gradually expands. When this user experience continues to accumulate significantly, then you know you are closer to being a producer than a user.

You now have an idea of what you need to study and learn. You can start proactively searching for the skills you need to start your own small business with near-zero capital or solve the problems of your struggling business. This is where Step 2 begins.

STEP 2. CREATE YOUR OWN CURRICULUM

It was in March 2020 that MKYU, the online college that I founded, started offering a business course for the first time: the Chief Instagram Officer (CIO) program that taught students the basics of Instagram and how to sell on it. I thought it would be a success if 500 people signed up for the program because it was a paid course, with a curriculum consisting of twenty lectures and weekly assignments, and students would complete the course only when they submitted the final assignment.

However, when registration began, the reaction was explosive. Nearly 1,900 students registered for the course. The students' enthusiasm was also tremendous once the program started. More than 1,000 assignments were submitted after each lecture, and students voluntarily put together study groups to question one another, provide one another with answers, and share the latest information and know-how.

Most of those who enrolled in the CIO program were career women or stay-at-home mothers between the ages of thirty-five and fifty-five. Many of them were nearly illiterate when it came to digital technology, and the only way in which most of them had incorporated it into their lives was by shopping online, which they only did because they were too busy working or raising children. A testament to their lack of knowledge was the question that I received most frequently: "I don't have an Instagram account and I really don't know anything about social media. Am I still eligible to sign up for the program?"

They have been so enthusiastic about studying that they no longer have to ask this and other similar questions. Their biggest motivation was the desire to become the CEO of their own Instagram shop, while making money—even a small amount—by studying and working hard.

Now is a time when you can chase your dreams by immediately learning the skills that connect you to the world and applying them to your work. You can easily fill a gap of several years by learning from experts. With a curriculum that you create by reflecting on the countless mistakes made by those who started before you, you can make much faster progress than by studying on your own.

These days, there is a flood of online platforms, such as Udemy and Skillshare, that give you access to just-in-time education. There is a growing number of paid platforms, such as Masterclass, where you can listen to lectures by overseas experts and leading scholars. Thousands of free instructional videos on various topics are available on You-Tube and TED.com. We are living in an era where we have direct access to the world's top educational content from our own living rooms.

If your job is about business development or marketing, or

even if, like me, you are the head of a company, studying and learning digital marketing is essential. Marketing has gone completely digital over the past few years. From business development to product or service to performance reviews, everything is based on data. Today, there are many new digital marketing methods, such as growth marketing and agile marketing–terms that might sound foreign to you. Data tracking and using analysis tools such as Google Analytics are the most basic of all the skills that you need to know. Digital marketing can only be learned online from professionals currently working in the field because marketing trends are changing too fast to learn from texts. You can learn all these skills and knowledge at a relatively affordable price. If you invest about $100 a month, you will get the same results as you would from attending three or four schools.

This is a world where you can watch YouTube and learn anything that you want to apply to your life. Just searching deeply on the internet alone can yield a massive amount of knowledge that experts acquired by studying for years, and it is all available for free. There are many overseas academic channels, where skilled professionals do their best–even though they don't have many subscribers–to share premium content and teach their subjects for free.

That's why I always urge my subscribers to create their own "study room" on YouTube. I have set up a separate YouTube account for that purpose. Currently, I'm subscribed to more than eighty channels, including Oprah Winfrey Network (OWN), which belongs to my role model, Oprah Winfrey; *The Ellen Show*; Live Academy, where I learn English; an economic analysis channel; and a science information channel.

When I'm too busy to watch new videos uploaded on my subscription channels and want to watch them later, I press the Save button on the video and send it to my playlist. My playlist has categories, such as role model, English study, economics, science, philosophy, and many others. Together, they make up my own educational curriculum. That's how I stay connected to the many sources of knowledge that are now available all over the world. The key is to connect with them early and stay connected so that you recognize changes as quickly as possible, no matter how turbulent the times may be.

STEP 3. LEARN DIGITAL GRAMMAR

I started learning Python a couple of months ago. Python is a computer programming language that is now widely used in the IT industry, and it is mostly used for machine learning programs. When my employees heard that I was going to learn Python, they cried out in disbelief.

They said, "Learning English is hard enough; how can you

learn computer language on top of that? Why do you want to learn it anyway?"

I told them, "I'm going to write simple apps myself–that's why."

They asked, "Do you have any idea how difficult that is? Why do you want to do it yourself? You can just give the job to app developers."

I answered, "Being the leader of a company, I should know the basic language that the developers use so I can work with them to create the app that I want. How do you expect me to let developers know what I want when I don't know the language and cannot communicate with them? I can envision my business only as much as I know digital."

Lately, I have been channeling all my energy into the digital transformation of MKYU. I keep envisioning what will happen when digital technology is introduced to the existing educational format. I understand the broad concepts of big data and artificial intelligence, but I don't know their details and therefore cannot envision the end product that would result from using them. I want to develop an app version of MKYU, but I realize that even though I've seen many apps created by others, I don't know enough about the process to do it myself.

None of my employees knew anything more than I did either.

Given the situation, it seemed that it was going to be difficult for me to recruit good IT professionals, let alone understand what they were telling me. I thought that when you are the head of a company, you should at least be knowledgeable enough to have a conversation with employees about your core business.

That's how I started taking Python lessons once a week from a graduate student in her late twenties who was majoring in computer science. I started the lessons ever so confidently, but after just one class, I was humbled. As I should have expected, computer language was extremely complicated, and there was a lot to memorize. But while learning it, I gradually began to understand its language. The more I learned about what was going on behind the screen while I was watching videos on the internet and using apps, the more confident I became.

At the same time that I am studying Python, I am gaining a developer's perspective of the world as well. In our first class of coding, my tutor explained:

"So what Facebook was thinking here is…"

"What Google wants to show is…"

I had been busy clicking when I visited portal sites, but now that I was looking at them from the viewpoints of developers, I was able to get completely different interpretations and ideas. It was a shocking experience. And I was extremely envious of the developers. How many business ideas would I find if I could just see the world from their viewpoint?

Most of the high-tech companies that are changing the world, such as Facebook, Apple, and YouTube, are run by CEOs who used to be developers or who are at least as imaginative as developers. In the post-fourth industrial revolution world, you can envision and design business in the right way only when you understand digital on the same level as the people who produce the technologies. If you understand digital on the same level as consumers, you are likely to be stuck being a consumer all your life. I wanted to understand digital as though I were a producer, not a consumer. That's the reason I started learning the basic language, albeit only at an introductory level, so that I can know how this world is structured.

But the more I learn, the more I realize that there is no need to be intimidated by digital. No matter how great a technology is, it is useless if it is not used to create content. Suppose there are people who don't know much about technology but have been creating content for twenty years. If these people become determined to learn something new, they can demonstrate tremendous potential, perhaps much more than those who know only technology and have no experience. One of the characteristics of people who have been making a living at a business for a long time is that they are brave and quick-witted. As long as we don't fear technology, experienced people like me can accomplish more than those in their twenties, who are only technologically savvy.

Experts say that subjects like Python will soon become one of the "general studies" taught in schools. In fact, even elementary school students are learning coding as a basic skill. There is also an increasing number of private schools that teach coding to adults, and there are numerous Python lessons for career men and women or beginners in the online education communities. There is a growing number of other digital classes for adults, including "Blockchain Technology for Your Business" and "Data Science Made Easy."

The most impressive class that I've seen recently is "How to Make AI Automatic Investment Bots." It is an online class that you can take for a fee at the website Class101.com. The website claims that you can learn to make your own AI stock-investing bots if you take its online classes for twenty weeks. A stock-investment bot is a sort of artificial intelligence that automatically increases your assets by buying and selling stocks on your behalf, while you are at work or traveling. Imagine that! A world where you can build your own artificial intelligence just by investing twenty weeks!

Will the people who master that class build only stock-investment bots? I'm thinking that they will build numerous personalized bots that will automate their work or business. People claim that these days finding a competent developer is as hard as finding a specific star in the sky. But if you want to begin using artificial intelligence in your business, perhaps you can solve the problem by learning technology yourself. Even if you don't learn enough to write perfect programs, you might start to understand digital grammar. Such understanding might even inspire you to new visions.

Recently, I asked Professor In Ho from Korea University to create a curriculum for a digital technology class for the general public at MKYU. I was sure that he was going to ask me, "Why do you bother to teach that to the general public?" So I even had an answer ready when I reached out to him. But the professor's reaction was completely the opposite of what I had expected.

"Good idea. Even the general public should have a comprehensive understanding of digital technology. Going forward, the less access to technology, the harder it will be to maintain the standard of daily life, much less business. I believe your students will take flight as if they had wings once they learn digital technology on top of what they have already learned," he said.

Only when you understand digital grammar can you continue to make a living and chase your dreams. At fifty-seven, even I am learning Python. Anybody younger than I can do it, too.

CHAPTER 14

CREATE YOUR OWN "TEAM" THAT WILL GROW WITH YOU

Just-in-time education doesn't have to happen only through books, information, or videos. In my experience, the surest way to achieve the most drastic growth in a short period of time is to learn from people. People have special roles that can only be played by living, breathing humans. Books and newspapers give you information and inspiration about what you should learn to prepare for the future, but they aren't interactive. Nor can they give you the answers to your immediate questions. But people who have already taken the road that you want to take can give practical advice. They can immediately tell you at which point you fell and how to raise yourself up again because they have gone through their own failures and successes. People are the best teachers because they can provide new learners with the personalized education that they need.

So the important question is, with whom should you be connected? First, there are people who are already living the daily life that you want to live. There are people who have already attained all the things that you believe are too difficult or too far in the future for you to achieve. These are the kind of people who can make great mentors.

I have one such person in my life. Her name is Jeong-eun, and she was part of the team that developed a global hit game, *PlayerUnknown's Battlegrounds*. I first met Jeong-eun in 2019 and was full of curiosity about her. Not only was she successful, but she was the developer of the game *Battlegrounds*, which my daughter loves. Jeong-eun was a very smart woman who was creating a world of games. I had met her only once before, but when my company became desperate to introduce digital technology, I thought of her again. I thought she would be a great coach to help me develop a new app.

Jeong-eun had grown significantly during the months between our meetings. The previous year, she had created a game studio, and she was preparing to launch a service UX-specializing company and a game UX-specializing company this year, and a Finnish game studio next year. Even now, she is involved in experiments and research for UX for the next generations, in addition to consulting and incubating a number of ventures, game studios, and game UX for project teams. Whenever she is working on a project, she stays in a foreign country for about four months, during which time she builds new experiences and knowledge; participates in exhibition activities, with art as a medium; and constantly communicates with people with good philosophies. In short, she is a small giant who is doing her best to ensure that today's precious time matures into the social DNA that the next generations will carry on. She was also the teacher that our company needed to develop and implement our core project.

"I want to turn MKYU into a really cool app, and I wonder if you can give me some advice," I asked her. She responded:

> The key to this project is to find a good designer and developer who are just right for you. To do so, it would be good if you and other key staff of your company take the initiative for R&D first, and I would like to suggest sprint as the best technology to carry out this project. It's one of the service-design techniques developed by Google, and it is a wonderful process to discover and complete the ultimate value of service in a short period of time. It is all included, from ideas to solutions to prototyping, which is the stage where you make a sample of your service or product, to the final user-testing stage. I think that your starting goal should be matching the grains of a team, who will carry out the MKYU project within a short time.

I was familiar with the concept of sprint planning that

Jeong-eun introduced to me because in the winter of 2019, I had visited Seattle and interviewed Jake Knapp and John Zeratsky, coauthors of the book *Sprint*, which explained the sprint technique. When you have a team of fewer than seven people, whose mission is to efficiently resolve a difficult project within a short time, have them focus on that project for five working days and then generate the result of the project. This is called sprint.[32] Jeong-eun told me about various examples of small startups that had used the sprint technique. She said that messenger programs for work, such as Slack, and a hotel room-service robot, Relay, were also created using this sprint approach.

Jeong-eun stressed that what was most needed for the success of MKYU was "creating a team of excellent experts." She introduced me to young women in their thirties, who were acclaimed as the best in their fields, and we are sharing ideas while constantly communicating through Messenger. I learned a lot from watching Jeong-eun connecting experts online and off-line to come up with ideas and grow fast together. I also found out that their way of working was to achieve fast growth by sharing, without hesitation, the content that they possessed. They were "open sources" that shared their knowledge with developers around the world. I was not familiar with their way, but they were cool and wonderful.

32 Jake Knapp, John Zeratsky, and Braden Kowitz, *Sprint: How to Solve Big Problems and Test New Ideas in Just Five Days* (New York: Simon & Schuster, 2016).

Jeong-eun is more than ten years my junior, but she has already lived not once, but several times, the future that I want to have ten years from now. She works in ways that make me envious, and she utilizes digital technology as routinely as breathing, which I wish I could do. Thanks to Jeong-eun, I think I'm getting closer to becoming what she is now. There is nothing more precious than learning from people. The people whose daily lives are the future you want—those are the people that you need to seek out and meet. They are the people who will bring you closer to your dreams and future.

FIND PEOPLE WHO MAKE YOUR HEART RACE

There are a second kind of people you must meet: those who inspire you. These are the people who see a problem and think about all the fun that they will have solving it, instead of listing the reasons why it might be difficult or even impossible. That's exactly how it is with two young men I met recently. One of them is Byung-eun, who studied at a college in the United States, worked at Samsung, started his career as an Amazon seller, and has now developed a solid company called Vintorio. Another is Chang-hyun, who is Byung-eun's best friend and who has a unique résumé. An elite student who, while studying at Columbia University in the United States, developed a near-obsessive interest in the problems of Korea's English-education system. Upon returning to Korea, he founded a startup called Home-

Grown Native to find solutions to problems in this area. To these two young men, there is no boundary between work and life, and since meeting them on business matters, they have become my constant muses and inspirations, and my heart always races when I talk with them about business.

I expected my first meeting with them to last about an hour. We ended up talking for more than five. While talking about marketing, global stores, digital solutions, millennials' dreams, startups, marriage, romance, career, and anything else, our conversation flowed effortlessly. We exchanged opinions and personal stories, raised questions, and answered them. Honestly, it was the first passionate and refreshing conversation that I had had in a long time. They were more than twenty years my junior, and they grew up while watching things that I've never watched and lived through times that I've never experienced myself. Their brains were already digitally structured. Besides, they had easy access to global businesses because they'd lived over-seas for years.

For many years, my conversation partners were mostly my employees, and we had fun spontaneously exchanging ideas with one another. But these days, I hardly get any response from them because our company has been expanding its business lines so much that they know that they will be put in charge of something if they bring it up. But these two young men were different. They had no problem speaking up to express their opinions because they were talking about someone else's business. When I told them about my business problems, their eyes sparkled, and they began drawing and writing in their notebooks. We developed ideas together, while giving spontaneous presentations on the spot. We must have created a dozen business items while chatting for five hours. Afterward, I felt as though I had read at least twenty books. I realized that often having a conversation with people who have both passion and content can result in the most learning in the shortest time.

When you are connected with people who inspire you and make your heart race over your business, you are destined to grow fast. Colorless and scentless books and information cannot give you such instantaneous and spontaneous inspiration. Just look around, and you will find good people who can inspire you. You have only overlooked them up until now because, for all these years, you've never been desperate enough to look for them. When you become a new learner, you start noticing the kind of people that you need.

MEET PEOPLE FROM DIFFERENT INDUSTRIES

The third kind of people you should connect with are those who work in different industries than you. When you are with people whom you have known well for a long time, you have a lot in common with them, including what you know and what you don't know. It's difficult to share original ideas with them. When you meet people who are total strangers to you, as I did when I met Jeong-eun, you gain connections and access to other areas, while at the same time broadening the range of your ideas and imagination. You can practice developing your own business by taking advantage of strangers' fresh new set of ideas, as if you have entered their brains. In this way, you can also improve the quality of your own work faster and more significantly.

In the future, collaboration with people working in other fields will become essential, as the technology cycle keeps growing shorter and the job cycle changes rapidly as well. That's the reason that companies like Google and Amazon value teamwork, instead of having employees sit quietly at their desks and do their jobs well. The key to their teamwork is being good at collaborating with people who are different from you.

If, like me, you belong to an older generation, I strongly recommend that you proactively communicate with younger people. Millennials might hate company dinners, but that doesn't mean that they hate being with people. A growing number of young people are joining meaningful groups to learn, support, and encourage one another. They can be great digital mentors for us.

Just look around you, and you will see that there are many groups of people who study, learn, and grow together with others. Online communities for people who share the same interests and hobbies have already established themselves as a business model. Ironic as it is, meetings and clubs are growing more dynamically than ever, as society grows more individualized.

Of course, you may be reluctant to meet strangers. You wonder if it's really worth the trouble to travel a long distance to them for the sake of learning something new when you already have a full schedule. You cannot let this inner voice stop you. There's always something special in a place you go for the first time. The person you are about to meet could be a treasure trove. It is possible that that person has something amazing inside; you just need to crack them open and see inside them. What you find might solve all your problems or connect you to the people whom you need to meet in order to do so. You must go out and find that person. Then team up so you can learn from each other and grow together.

CHAPTER 15

‖‖‖‖‖‖‖‖‖‖‖‖‖

HABITS TO CREATE INSIGHTS INTO THE FUTURE

The last stage of just-in-time education for a new learner is getting into the habit of studying whatever information they come across. When the world changes as fast as it is now doing, people often turn to those who have been successful and ask them about the future. We believe that those with more experience have better insight. But I believe, without doubt, that it is hard work that gives us a successful, ful-filling life. Hard work never betrays. Those who are awake achieve more than those who are asleep, and those who keep the door wide open in order to understand can learn much more than those who keep their doors and ears closed. You cannot find solutions to your problems if you do not seek knowledge everywhere.

Insight is the ability to quickly make the best choices that you need to make in order to be successful and happy. People with good insights are the ones who know what to choose to achieve these goals. People say that I have good insight and am quick-witted. So I'm often asked to help people improve their insight. Regretfully, I cannot give people insight because different individuals have very different ways of seeing the world, dreaming, growing, and achieving success.

Now that the world is changing so rapidly, you must find your own insight. Developing insight begins by collecting the information around you, studying it, and using it as a guide to achieving your dreams. Only then can you move in a direction where you can fulfill yourself in the ways that you want and that suit you best. To help you do this, I am going to help you learn how to diligently study the information available to you. Once you get into the habit of studying a wide range of information, you can develop your own insight and succeed in the world.

READING HELPS US UNDERSTAND THE FUTURE AS THE PRESENT REALITY

Books are indispensable when you want to get into the habit of studying. Since I've uploaded to my YouTube channel so many videos about how to overcome the coronavirus crisis, my subscribers often say to me, "I want to start studying now to prepare for the post-coronavirus world, but I don't know which book to start reading. Please recommend a book for me."

At first, I didn't know what to say because I've read so many books over the past few months. But after reading hundreds, I began to recognize a theme that ran through the books that I had read.

The books that I read in the beginning covered various ways to deal with a crisis, including *Upheaval: How Nations Cope with Crisis and Change* by Jared Diamond and *Factfulness* by Hans Rosling, Ola Rosling, and Anna Rosling Rönnlund. I also read books authored by world-renowned scholars that discussed future society as a whole, such as *21 Lessons for the 21st Century* by Yuval Harari and *Mastering Megatrends* by Doris Naisbitt and John Naisbitt. I also read novels, including George Orwell's *1984* and *Neuromancer* by William Gibson. When you are looking for the major trends that will define the future, you need to put the present into context, determining where our present state fits into all of human history. Two of the books that deal with this subject are Yuval Harari's *Sapiens* and *Homo Deus*. They can help you connect the past, present, and future of humankind.

If you can see the big picture of the world ahead of us, now is the time to study the specifics of the future of digital technology. In bookstores, there are abundant books dealing with artificial intelligence, big data, blockchains, Internet of Things, robots, and so on. If you read recent releases on these subjects, you will begin to notice frequently used terms. Books that address economic trends should also be on your reading list. I recommend that you study everything that is closely related to your livelihood, such as the changes that are likely to occur in corporations, the job market, and finance.

Books about the companies that will spearhead the future and the CEOs of those companies are also useful. If you read real business stories about Jeff Bezos of Amazon, Mark Zuckerberg of Facebook, and Elon Musk of Tesla, you will understand how both their successes and failures helped them get one step ahead of others. While "conversing" with them through books, you will find clues that can be applied to your life.

You don't have to read these books in the same order that I read them. Start by first reading the book that is of most interest to you, and don't feel pressured to read them all. What matters is that you start to read. As you read one book, you will begin to identify others that elaborate on the theme that you see emerging. The more you read on the subjects that will prepare you for the future, the faster you will learn which knowledge and skills you are going to need to prepare you for the times ahead. The minute that you realize that all the things you doubted would ever happen already exist, the faster your life will change and you will find opportunities that you never even imagined.

BELIEVE IN YOUR INSIGHT AND REMAIN UNSHAKEN

What I want to emphasize here is that you need to get into the habit of collecting information about coming changes. You need to get into the habit of finding information from as many sources as possible, including news articles, books, and other people. Getting into the habit of collecting information and interpreting it helps you find opportunities in a changing world, but more importantly, it helps you keep your life centered.

It won't be long before we start hearing about windfalls: a company attracting big investors, the founder of a small startup joining the billionaires' club, or somebody who once worked with you going independent and raking in money. The news about companies and individuals who have jumped on changes when they were rapidly happening in an uncertain world deserves applause, but on the other hand, that kind of news might make you feel very small and insignificant, as you quietly follow the path of your choice. Suddenly, you are not sure if you have taken the right path, and the more you question your choice, the more you become withdrawn and lose confidence.

That's why you need insight. Your insight is the only thing

that protects you. Your confidence is the only thing that will help you keep moving forward toward the future, while moving at the pace that suits you best and dreaming dreams that will be possible in the new world. Others' success makes you want to stop working to gain insight, and it shakes your conviction. You feel as though you should abandon the path that you have chosen and follow that of others, and therefore you keep getting distracted and tempted to listen to what others are saying. You want to borrow someone else's way of success as soon as you can. You need insight in order to keep your balance.

In my book *MK Kim's Dream On*, published in 2013, I stressed the importance of not dreaming someone else's dreams. Your dreams must be made by you. You must not shop for your dreams. You should never pick dreams that look good to you—as if they were products on display in a department store—and make them yours. Since other people's dreams did not come from you, they aren't a good fit for you. They don't help you to fulfill yourself, and worse, you might end up devoting your life to chasing after somebody else's dreams.

It's been nearly a decade since I wrote my book, and the same rule applies to success as it does to dreams. It is your job to decide what you should do and how you should make a living in accordance with the four formulas of the post-coronavirus world. It is insight that helps you choose the best answer for you. Ultimately, you are the one to make and build the insight that makes you understand the world and moves you. Insight doesn't happen unless you follow a diligent method.

Insight is not a spiritual language but a physical language. You can tell yourself, "I want to become a decent person" or "I want to be a very awakened person," but that doesn't accomplish anything, even if you repeat it a hundred times. Insight grows as much as you physically confront, struggle, and battle with issues whenever they arise. I advised you to read newspapers, trend reports, and books, but don't mistake them for *mental* labor. I've stood and read newspapers for two hours every morning, I've read thousands of pages of reports every night while fighting sleepiness, and I've read hundreds of books. All of this has been purely *physical* labor. All the pieces of information that I acquired can pass through my mind and ferment to become fit for my use only through physical labor.

Do you want to overcome the anxiety that you feel because of the mistakes that you've made in the past and the fear that you have of the new, unknown future? Then what you need is to immediately start building a habit that helps you grow your insight. Studying is not something you do when you are young and have a ton of extra time. The studying you do when life is hard and you are desperate can truly become the driving force of your life. The first week or so will be difficult, but just keep going, and after about a year, you will find a new you, who has extraordinary insight.

PART 5

PHILOSOPHY OF COEXISTENCE

NEW HUMANS WILL SAVE THE FUTURE

Coronavirus will be over someday. And we'll survive. I hope that when it happens, our children will think of consideration and trust, not distrust.

I hope they will choose courage instead of hatred. To make this happen, we grown-ups must support and encourage one another. I hope that even in times of disaster such as coronavirus, we will be able to reach out, comfort one another, and say, "It must be harder on you than on me."

The survival of a relationship and the survival of trust are just as important as the survival of our lives.

CHAPTER 16

‖‖‖‖‖‖‖‖‖‖‖‖‖‖‖‖‖

CLIMATE CHANGE

THE LAST GOLDEN HOUR AVAILABLE TO US

I'm not an ecology activist, a nature conservation expert, or an animal lover. I am just one of the ordinary people who feels guilty when I put out too much food, waste, or recyclables on garbage pickup day and who tried to redeem my guilt by using eco-friendly dish soap. That's how I used to be, but now I have changed. I bring reusable bags, which I have never done before, when I go grocery shopping, and I choose eco-friendly products even though they are on the pricey side. Out of concern over plastic bottle-waste issues, I gave up my habit of drinking bottled water and now I carry a tumbler with me in my bag. I choose to walk when I go places if they are not too far, and I listed my car on the used-car market because now that I don't have a speaking schedule, I don't need a car. Every time I meet somebody, I tend to have a heated debate over the seriousness of climate change and environmental problems in general.

If you ask me what's up with all these sudden changes, I will tell you it was because of COVID-19. It pained me to think that I could not go back to the daily routines I had in the past, when I could go places freely and didn't have to wear a mask to meet somebody–all because of COVID-19. The more I dug deeper into the cause of the pandemic, the more it was difficult to shake off the thought that the virus was nature's warning to us humans.

Is this the only crisis that we will have to deal with? Isn't it possible that this crisis is only a prelude to a much bigger disaster? Will we be able to pull through if a crisis more dangerous than the virus strikes?

One day in March, when the coronavirus was in full swing, I discovered a movie that described our current situation. The 2011 film *Contagion* could have been made today. There were uncanny parallels between the film and the current pandemic situation, including the fact that zoonotic disease started in bats in Malaysia.

In the movie, the first confirmed case is traced to a restaurant in Hong Kong, where a pig that had eaten the manure of bats was cooked and served. Before long, a staggering number of confirmed cases were reported along the flow of the virus carriers' traffic in airports, buses, hotels, and houses, before the virus spread around the world in a flash. The movie goes on to show how it is possible for humans to change into monsters when faced with a contagious virus, as people struggle to control the virus through such measures as self-isolation, tracing, shutdowns, mass burials, severed human relationships, suspicion of others to the level of terror, and the selfish instinct for survival. In fact, the movie described exactly what is happening today.

WE ARE THE ROOT CAUSE OF CORONAVIRUS

In fact, we have already heard so much about humans' destruction of the environment that by now it is a familiar problem to us. But I don't think that we have ever taken it seriously as something that directly affected us. Then I came upon the column "An Old Disease Caused by Humans," contributed by an environmental philosopher, Woo Seok-young, to the *Hankyoreh* newspaper on March 27, 2020. Reading this column, I got a hint of how we can make a living in this stringent time:

> Since the 1980s, climate scientists have talked about the seriousness of climate change, and some ecologists, historians, and infectious disease experts have raised their voices about the risk of new infectious diseases. In the 1920s, a few ignorant people ate chimpanzee meat and exposed themselves to a virus that chimpanzees were carrying. This

virus came to be known as AIDS. In 1976, the virgin forests by the Ebola River in the Congo were destroyed, and the consequential contact between humans and wildlife resulted in the outbreak of a virus with a death rate of 88 percent. This was Ebola. Tragedy continues. In 1998, the virus was transferred from boars to humans in Malaysia. It happened because humans forayed into the woods to expand their pig farms. The cause was believed to have been pieces of fruit that were dropped by bats and eaten by boars. There are many other contagious diseases, and humans are always found in the background of most of these diseases. We must quickly wake up to the fact that the more we destroy the forest and disrupt the conditions of Nature, the greater the danger we will be exposed to.[33]

Human destruction of the environment was the cause of all these infectious diseases. Jeremy Rifkin, the most influential social thinker and futurist of our time, recently claimed in an interview with the media that climate change was the cause of all these pandemics.[34] He pinned the blame on the destruction of the ecosystem that had resulted from the disrupted circulation of water, human invasions of wildlife's territories, and the consequential migration of the wildlife.

---

33 Seok-young Woo, "An Old Disease Caused by Humans," *Hankyoreh*, March 27. 2020, http://www.hani.co.kr/arti/animalpeople/human_animal/934468.html (translated to English from source in Korean).

34 Jeremy Rifkin, "Coronavirus Is a Pandemic Caused by Climate Change: We Will Fall Together unless We Solve Together," interview by Ahn Hee-Kyung, Kyunghyang Shinmun, May 14, 2020, http://news.khan.co.kr/kh_news/khan_art_view.html?art_id=202005140600005 (translated to English from source in Korean).

He also predicted that more infectious diseases will strike us in the future. It is terrifying just to hear his account.

- A massive wildfire broke out in the state of New South Wales in southeastern Australia and turned an area larger than that of South Korea into darkness.
- More than 7,000 forest fires occur each year in California in the United States.
- Even Alaska, which is located in the northern hemisphere, is scorching under heat waves, causing mass deaths of seabirds.
- Most countries in Europe are suffering from heat waves. The Netherlands and Belgium recorded their highest temperatures of 40°C for the first time in their history.
- India sustained serious human casualties and economic damage due to an extreme spell of drought. The City of Chennai hasn't had any rain for 196 days.

These are not plot lines from movies. These are abnormal weather phenomena that I read about in the "2019 Abnormal Weather Report" published by the Korea Meteorological Administration.[35] The above-listed situations account for only a small part of the whole reality. All different kinds of natural disasters, such as heat waves, droughts, wildfires,

---

35 Korea Meteorological Administration, "2019 Abnormal Weather Report," accessed February 11, 2021, http://www.climate.go.kr/home/bbs/view.php?code=93&bname=abnormal&vcode=6385 (translated to English from source in Korean).

floods, and hurricanes are occurring more frequently and intensely than ever.

Does that mean that the conclusion is already drawn? Are we left with no more golden hour? Scientists argue that global warming was an expected result. According to them, as a result of our competitive race toward abundance over the past thirty years, the environment on earth is becoming too perilous for humans to inhabit.

David Wallace-Wells, in his book *The Uninhabitable Earth: Life after Warming*, argues that climate change is not a moral fable, and "unless we choose to halt it, it will never stop." Wallace-Wells also writes that how the future of our climate will play out is full of uncertainty, which "emerges not from scientific ignorance but, overwhelmingly, from the open question of how we respond."[36]

In other words, it is a question that should be answered by humans, not natural science, because, according to Wallace-Wells, the most important factor at this stage is how much carbon we put into the atmosphere. Of course, "we" refers to none other than us; it refers to our generation, who are inhabiting the earth now. It will be too late if we put it off to the next generation.

---

36 David Wallace-Wells, *The Uninhabitable Earth: Life after Warming* (New York: Tim Duggan Books, 2020).

CHILDREN TO BE LEFT IN A HELLISH WORLD

I feel sorry whenever I see children going to school wearing masks these days. I belong to the generation that hit the jackpot in the "birth lottery" and won the right to enjoy the resources of planet Earth to their fullest. When I was young, I ran around on beautiful roads lined with cosmos flowers, and in summer I hung out with my friends in mountains and fields, where there was an abundance of wild berries and acacia honey for us to pick and eat everywhere. In autumn, we had field days without having to worry about fine dust, and in winter we scooped up a handful of acid-free snow and ate it deliciously.

Now, all these memories are available only in photos of history books. In spring, our children can't go out and play or hang out with friends, and when going to school, they have to wear masks. This has become their daily routine, and it's all because of fine dust. It is already heartbreaking enough that our generation passed on to them an environment that has been polluted due to our reckless abuse of the natural resources. Now they have become the "corona generation" and must live with the scars left by COVID-19. Our children will not be able to enjoy—even if they are willing to pay for them—all the happy daily routines that our generation enjoyed without having to pay the price. They might even have to live in a horrific world where they will have to pay even for water and air for survival.

The current situation is hard to swallow even for me, who has already lived half my life, and I cannot imagine how unfair and frustrating it will be for our children, who will have to live in a natural environment that has been devastated due to our mistakes. I realized that our children are already feeling the same way, when I read a news article about some teenagers having filed a constitutional petition against the Korean government. Kim Yujin, along with twenty-nine other young activists, stated that "their fundamental rights, including the right to live in a clean environment, have been infringed on by the nation's climate-change law," which is not specific enough to prevent global temperatures from rising.[37]

The kids' frustrated appeal is an earnest request for help to save them from the government and grown-ups, who turn blind eyes to such a serious climate-change problem and are not taking any measures to do something about it. They know that unless somebody does something immediately, their future will be nothing short of hell.

Fortunately, however, people's awareness of climate change has started to grow since we've been hit by the coronavirus. According to a survey of 1,000 men and women, conducted in April 2020 by the Center for Environmental Health and

---

37 Heesu Lee, "'We Want Drastic Change': South Korean Teens Sue Government to Demand Bigger Cut in Emissions," *Time*, March 12, 2020, https://time.com/5802264/ south-korea-teens-sue-government-climate-change/.

Citizens, 86 percent of the respondents answered that the root cause of COVID-19 was climate change, which is responsible for the spread of the virus that causes zoonotic contagious disease.[38] It is a big relief because the fact that people believe our environmentally destructive behaviors are the cause of the contagious disease gives us hope that we might be able to solve the problem that we are now facing.

Lately, the Korean government also announced the Green New Deal policy to create new jobs dedicated to finding solutions to climate change, such as reducing greenhouse gas emissions. Finally, it seems that we can see a flicker of hope. Had it not been for the coronavirus, would we have reached a consensus on the need to respond to the climate change issue so quickly? I even think that coronavirus might be a messenger that reached out to us in order to prevent a bigger disaster.

Korea's leading ecologist, Prof. Choi Jae-Cheon, names Pak Kyongni, a novelist and mother figure for every Korean, as the person he admires most. He talks about what she said whenever he has a chance. He says that his favorite quote of hers was, "Humans should live off the interest incurring from Nature's principal only."

---

38   Yu-seung Kim, "Survey: Most Important Environmental News This Year Is COVID-19," News1 Korea, December 23, 2020, https://www.news1.kr/articles/?4159901 (translated to English from source in Korean).

Nature is not infinite. The earth's resources are too limited to accommodate humans' endless desires. Let's say nature is our bank account. We should have been moderate with how much we withdrew from it in order to keep the account in good standing. But we kept taking out of the account, and as if that weren't enough, we even took loans from nature, using our children's future as collateral. The result is that nature is nearly drained and has almost nothing left, including what should have been our children's share.

Now we should start paying back. We must pay back what we borrowed, and it would be great if we could afford to start saving as well. This is not a matter of choice: it's the debt that our generation must pay.

All parents want to dress and feed their children well and educate them to ensure that they find a good job and have a comfortable life. But all this is possible only if we remain alive. If climate change accelerates its progress until earth becomes no longer habitable, it will be meaningless to dream of a good life.

THREE THINGS YOU NEED TO START DOING IMMEDIATELY

So the question is, what should we do right now? To find the answer, I read reference books and reached out to experts in the areas of the environment, climate change, and humanities, as well as to philosophers for their advice. As a result, I managed to find three answers that I was looking for.

1. LEAVE SOME FOR OTHERS

If you think only of now and your own satisfaction, you tend to use things more than necessary. There is only one thing we can do to slow down future disasters, and that is using less of everything. The environment that has been ruined by 7.7 billion people must be compensated for by 7.7 billion people. The future of our children is something we cannot leave to somebody's responsibility. In the worst-case scenario, children born in 2020 may have to live in a harsh environment for their entire lives. We must ask and answer a question every day as long as we live: "Am I going to leave my children a land laden with pain and despair?"

Let's stop shifting our responsibility to ecologists or environmentalists. Rather, we must be more responsible and proactive regarding environmental issues, particularly if we are raising children. The years when you have been aloof to environmental issues out of ignorance should be enough to make you feel ashamed of yourself. But if you start acting immediately, you can slow down the clock that is ticking toward doomsday.

There is nothing difficult about it. You just need to ask yourself a few more questions when you go grocery shopping:

"Do I really have to buy this?"; "Shouldn't I buy eco-friendly products even though they are on the pricey side?"; "Wouldn't I be contributing to protecting the environment if I avoided buying anything wrapped with Styrofoam?"; and "Wouldn't I help prolong earth's life expectancy if I bought fruit damaged slightly by bugs?" You can make a difference if you just build "eco-friendly daily routines" like these, making all decisions by using the eco-friendliness filter.

I started my own ecological routine a while ago. "Please put it in a tumbler instead of a disposable cup." "I don't need another bag; I'll put it in my own." That's how I suck up a little inconvenience and make it a habit to carry a tumbler and reusable bags with me to minimize the use of disposable products as much as I can. It doesn't have to be extraordinary. We can practice environment-saving consumption just by making small adjustments in our daily lives.

We have been turning blind eyes to environmental issues and outsourcing the solutions for many years. We've been shifting our responsibilities to recycling companies and the government, expecting them to do something to take care of the outcomes of our carelessness. We've never listened to the warnings of environmentalists and ecologists. We can no longer rely on others to deal with the problems. It is time for us to fulfill our share of responsibilities by developing the habit of consuming less before it's too late.

2. SPEND MORE NOW TO REAP THE BENEFITS LATER

A while ago, I was having a conversation with Professor Choi Jae-Cheon. He told me, "I've been telling people over and over again that if we continue to damage nature, we may get what we want right now, but in the long run, we will end up losing more economically. But nobody listened to me. So I developed a new theory called Environmental Economics by consulting with economists. It is a new frame that says, 'Environmental problems are economic problems.'"

I thought, "Companies will finally listen to him now that he has gone this far." But as was expected, companies only pretended they were listening to him by just making small donations for his cause. Ecological and environmental issues have always been pushed to the side in favor of development. But I have no doubt that things will be different now because people have realized that the key to solving the coronavirus problem can be found not in masks or vaccines but in the environment. People have also started realizing, deep within, that it is a problem for us all, not others, to solve. There are things that people can do individually, but companies that leave a massive impact on the environment with just one round of their production activity should also do something to solve this problem.

Now is the time when companies and small businesses should be called on to put in place guidelines for environmental protection and even climate change when they do business or sell products. It is the consumer's job to commend products that were made while taking the environment into consideration. We must spend more money for the healthy future of our children now, instead of saving it. Electricity and oil consumption should be cut down, but eco-friendly products should be our first choice, even though they are slightly more expensive than others. The more money we spend now, the more we will be investing in the future wellness of our children.

I was heavy hearted the entire time I interviewed Professor Choi Jae-Cheon. I was so sorry for not having acknowledged all the hard work and efforts that environmental protection activists have been making all these years on our behalf. So when Professor Choi Jae-Cheon told me that the Biodiversity Foundation that had been founded was short of funding and might have to lay off employees, I blurted out almost instinctively,

"Professor, I will also sponsor the Biodiversity Foundation."

When the video of me interviewing Prof. Choi was uploaded onto my YouTube channel, MKTV, it touched the hearts of many of my subscribers. A short while later, I received a text message from Professor Choi Jae-Cheon. He said that many people had started sponsoring the foundation, and he thanked me. It was such a significant relief to hear it because it made me feel that the world was still a good place to live.

And I was grateful for being a part of the community that demonstrated such mature citizenship.

3. PUT UP WITH A LITTLE INCONVENIENCE

When you think about it, we are living in an era where everything is abundant. We use electricity and water as much as we want to. It's because they are cheap. I wondered why they were cheap, and I realized that it was because we've been exploiting natural resources that should have been reserved for the future. We cared only about our convenience here and now, and we didn't think about the dangers that we'll face later on in the future.

Now the bills we pay should include the "inconvenient cost." The price is right when the inconvenient cost of reduction is added to the bill. We must recalculate our bill, adding the interest incurred to the resources we've been using for our convenience.

I recently came to learn that an organization called the Korea Climate and Environment Network has for many years been carrying out a campaign to "reduce one ton of carbon per one person."[39] I was conscience-stricken while reading the statements on the campaign website because they were

---

39 Korea Climate and Environment Network, "Reducing One Ton of GHG per Person," accessed February 11, 2021, http://www.kcen.kr/eng/lowCarbon/life. jsp;jsessionid=2221C213B16E43DBF8485A0F4005FCB4.

mainly addressed to children, and there were more photos than texts. Environmental education was more necessary to us, grown-ups, but I felt that we had passed on that load to our innocent children.

Aren't we supposed to finish what we have started and work harder than ever to do it? What we need is to practice accepting our share of "beautiful inconvenience" by using AC and vehicles less, using the most-energy-efficient appliances, unplugging electric cords when not in use, wasting less food scraps, and saving water.

"It's a little inconvenience, but I'll drive less."

"It's a little inconvenience, but I'll use electricity only when it is necessary."

"It's a little inconvenience, but I'll use water sparingly."

These slogans might sound like those that you put on posters when you were an elementary school student, but considering the reality in which we are living, it seems right for us to start from this level. After all, we are only on the level of toddlers when it comes to this area.

Still, I am extremely ashamed of myself for having been so negligent about environmental issues, considering how I've been training people and suggesting solutions and delivering messages for close to thirty years. If we adults got down to business in earnest, I'm sure that we could come up with thousands of ideas, and I've been thinking hard to figure out what I can do myself to contribute to the environment-saving campaign. If I could take a guess, I am highly likely to participate in the campaign by delivering speeches and offering training programs because that's what I do best.

There is no future for us unless we are determined to live with small inconveniences. We must recognize that Earth is not going to end after our generation; it is a world that we will pass on to the next generation so that they can live here. Only when we change our ways will we be able to guarantee happiness and safety for our children on Earth.

"All tragedies carry hidden messages within."

This is something I believe and, in fact, count on to be true. Whenever life throws me a curveball, I try to read "the message that will enlighten me," that is hidden behind the trouble I am facing. I tell myself, "Why did this misfortune strike me? There must be a reason. I should find it."

The coronavirus also sent me off balance because it was a crisis like none that I've ever experienced in my entire life. But before long, I found the hidden message that told me to be prepared for a bigger misfortune. Perhaps the current situation could be sending a message to us from the children of the future. How fortunate it is to realize it, be it so belatedly.

Consuming less and leaving more for future generations is a duty that we need to fulfill in the wake of the coronavirus crisis.

CHAPTER 17

THREE VACCINES TO BUILD STRONGER MENTAL IMMUNITY

There are times in our lives when we become sick at heart. We put up with cuts and scratches that we sustain in our daily lives, but when we get sick at heart, there are two causes: serious health problems or money problems. When people unexpectedly get diagnosed with cancer, or when failed businesses leave them in deep debt, they suffer from extreme stress and even mental illness.

Now, however, we are exposed to these two biggest causes of mental sickness at once. Just the fear over getting the virus and dying from it is in itself nerve wracking, but to it has been added a crumbling financial foundation. Everything that we've been doing up until now and the foundation of our livelihoods are suddenly crumbling, as if the ground is splitting and swallowing everything after being hit by an earthquake. This is a situation that leaves us most vulnerable to mental illness. In a recent survey, seven out of ten respondents answered that they experienced depression and anxiety caused by what is called the corona blues.

What we need in this case is mental immunity. Immunity, or our body's power to fight disease, is not needed just for physical illnesses. We need immunity to save ourselves from mental illness. In the past, we had many options to turn to when we were depressed or sad. We could meet friends and talk, go to movies, or even have a getaway. Those little things were fun, while at the same time healing us, but now that they have been taken away from us, we are feeling all the more frustrated and lost.

The hope that it will subside soon is also fading. Even with the arrival of the vaccines, it is certainly taking longer to be resolved than what most people would want or hope. Even those with an iron heart become vulnerable to despair and devastation, and they question themselves: "What have I done so far?" Now that you have to live with depression, anxiety, and heartache, you need more than just an ordinary heart. It is difficult to maintain the pre-coronavirus mindset post-coronavirus. If you want to make it through day after day with a smile—even a forced one—no matter how challenging the situation is and remain unfazed in the face of change–no matter how unexpected–you must develop stronger mental immunity.

I already have fifty-seven years of experience in life, but even for me, this coronavirus crisis was not easy to take. I was devastated at the beginning of the crisis, even though I've never doubted my mental immunity and resilience for recovery. My mind kept leaning toward depression and anxiety, even though I didn't do anything. There is something I told myself whenever I found myself in this poor shape. When I think about it, this word could have been the vaccine for my heart.

WHEN YOU'VE GOT SOMETHING THAT DAUNTS YOU, FOLD IT INTO HALF THE SIZE

"This technology is not a big deal. I can master this in just a year, considering all my life experience."

That's what I've told myself whenever I felt daunted by digital technology. I guess I must have said it to myself at least a dozen times a day. It is natural for anybody to feel intimidated when trying something new or going to a place for the first time. I am confident in almost all other parts of my life, but when I dipped my toe into the digital world, I found myself intimidated in spite of myself. The terms also horrified me because they were all English acronyms and newly coined words, which looked to me like an alien language:

blockchain, digital money, AI, ICT, IoT, among numerous others. It took me a long time just to figure out what these strange-sounding terms meant and to get myself used to them. I couldn't help but admire those who were using these terms routinely, without any trouble.

We often overestimate the things that we don't have. And we think that those who understand what we don't are amazingly smart. We even feel inferior to those who seem to be much smarter and who are moving far ahead of us. It is natural to feel that way because, after all, we are only human, but we must not let ourselves be imprisoned by such thoughts. We must not let our hearts keep shrinking smaller and smaller.

From now on, we must go through the process of integrating digital technologies with our work. It is an inevitable process to survive in the post-coronavirus era. But it frightens you because there is so much to study, and you are not even familiar with the language. Whenever that happened to me, I folded in half what I needed to attack and made it half its original size. It has been my way of intentionally underestimating what I need to tackle.

"It's just a digital technology and not a big deal if I study a little harder. I'm not an idiot, am I? Of course, others are better than me because they had a head start by studying it several years ahead of me!"

Of course, I could be so audacious because I had the foundational conviction about myself. Conviction happens when you keep building basic life skills over a long period of time. For years, you have been building the analog skills that you use in your work, the skills that have been supporting you for the past ten years, while you were working in the analog world: if you are a teacher, good teaching skills; if you are a salesperson, the skill to make good connections and sell products or services; and if you are a restaurant owner, the skills of writing recipes, developing menus, running a business, and even marketing and promoting your business. You have survived until now because you had those respective skills. And those skills were not given to you overnight; you've been building and honing them over a long time, while undergoing numerous trials, errors, and failures. Those skills are your unique assets, but at this point, people underestimate the skills that they've been building throughout their lives.

People think that the skills they have are not a big deal because others have as much skill to support themselves. But skill is never "not a big deal." If you've been making enough money to provide for yourself and your family in such a fiercely competitive society, the skills that you have acquired and used to make a living all these years have already proven their value. Your skills aren't going anywhere just because the world is going digital. You carry them with you as you move on.

What really matters for us in life is skill, not technique. In the case of technique, you can master it within a short time if you apply yourself to it. You can master the basic techniques you need for your business in just a few months if you are determined. But skill is something that you can only get after years of sharpening and honing, and it is the real core content that will feed you and provide for you.

We must not miss this important distinction. Without the basic skills we need to make a living, techniques are useless. If I didn't have the skill to speak as I do, I doubt that anybody would listen to me. You may know all the techniques to promote your business on social media, but your business cannot last long if the food you serve is not delicious or if you don't know how to run a business. You may apply agile marketing to quickly analyze big data and evaluate business performance, but if the quality of the product that you are selling is substandard, you cannot sell it, no matter what and how hard you try.

Besides, most of the techniques that are introduced these days have a short life cycle. In just two years or so, another technique is introduced to replace the old one. Given that, if we are reluctant to jump in and learn techniques now, we will never learn them. Therefore, we can start slowly by learning the basics of new techniques, just as we would when learning English. Techniques may seem far out there in the beginning, but once you start using them, they become just another part of your life. Stop being intimidated. When you are feeling small in the face of new techniques, and when somebody is on a roll with the support of digital technology, keep giving yourself pep talks instead of being intimidated. Keep practicing and encouraging yourself. Take time to acknowledge your competency. You have been working hard for all these years, and you deserve it.

BEAT THE CHAOS VARIABLE WITH AN UNCHANGING CONSTANT

Coronavirus has forced us to revise our life plans one way or another. Some have had to give up their post-retirement goals, some have lost the channels through which they export their goods, and some have had their future dreams crushed. But just because you have had to give up your dreams and plans doesn't mean that you are justified in sitting and waiting forever. If your post-retirement plan has been ruined, you can start making another plan with a new goal; if you have lost the channels through which you export goods, revamp your business portfolio; and if it has become impossible for you to realize your dreams, you must find a detour by which you can reach them. In short, if you want to find the path to the dreams and plans that you have lost during the coronavirus, you must modify your goals. That's the only way.

The first thing to do when modifying your goal is to distinguish between constants and variables. If you remain determined to do a particular kind of work, no matter how the world and circumstances surrounding you change, you are the constant. All the variables, other than yourself, can be modified if you wish. If you confuse the constants with the variables, you are likely to fail.

A while ago, a friend of mine who is the mother of a college student, called me and lamented. She said that her son was supposed to go to Australia for a working-holiday program the previous month, but his plans had been foiled, and now he was so disappointed that he didn't do anything all day other than lying down and looking at his smartphone.

The circumstance that foiled his plan to go for the working-holiday program is a variable. Variables can always be replaced with other variables. If he looks for it, there are ways to learn English while making money. But if he mistakes the changed circumstance as being an unchanging constant, he is bound to be disappointed about not being able to go for the working holiday. He is being trapped by external factors that are not within his power to change, instead of looking for a solution that revolves around the most important factor: himself. However, if he can distinguish which is a constant and which is a variable, he could think, "How fortunate that I didn't go to Australia because I could have gone there only to be locked down because of coronavirus."

At a time such as now, when everything changes drastically, you must be able to create scenarios that have you, the most important constant, at their center. Only then can you find the right path to take. In the current situation, you must take the initiative to modify and change all the variables around you in order to keep the constant that is you. If it is hard to find what is best for you, you should try to find what is next best for you. When you pull yourself together in this way, you can live in the changing world as a meaningful being. Who knows? Perhaps this is the best time for you to reflect on yourself and find better dreams—ones that are more fitting for you.

If there is one thing I have come to realize after living for more than fifty years, it is the fact that you cannot change anything just by blaming the circumstances of your life. There are two kinds of circumstances in life: one is fortune, and the other is misfortune. If fortune is about getting everything that you wish for, misfortune is about not getting what you want, no matter how you try. Now, however, when I look back at my life, I realize that none of the things that I have experienced had anything to do with fortune or misfortune. Whatever happened to me was all colorless, scentless, and neutral, and there was no inherent intention in it. It became either fortune or misfortune, depending on how I dealt with the situation at the time.

The current situation becomes a little clearer when you treat coronavirus as a circumstance. How about perceiving the pandemic as a circumstance that may bring you fortune, instead of definitively defining it as a misfortune. Who knows? Perhaps sometime in the future you will be able to say, "Back then, coronavirus ruined all my plans. I thought it was a misfortune, but now I realize that it was a fortune because it gave me an opportunity to rid myself of all that that was behind the times and start my business with a new approach."

In fact, I also have to revise all the plans I had for 2021. I had plans to stay in the United States, Europe, and Vietnam for three months each to speak and take intensive English classes, but all these plans had to be scrapped. Can I call this situation a fortune or a misfortune? Whenever I wonder about it, I tell myself, "Coronavirus is just a variable. Fortunately, both my company and I are in good shape, so that's okay. I should just take a deep breath and do my best doing what I can now."

One thing is clear: just because things didn't go the way you'd planned doesn't mean it is a misfortune. A real misfortune is when your road is blocked–your plans are foiled and your dreams are crushed–and you fail to look for another path.

For some people, coronavirus may seem to be a "pause" button that stops them from doing anything. But if you change the angle of your perspective slightly, it can be a new opportunity that lets you dream "another dream." Instead of letting yourself (a constant) feel devastated by the coronavirus (a variable), use new strengths, ones that you haven't used before, instead of despairing and doing nothing. As you go through difficult times, constantly remind yourself that you are the master of your life.

I CANNOT IMAGINE HOW HARD IT MUST BE FOR YOU

The last word that touched me like a vaccine for my mind came from someone else that I knew.

One day, I called him and said, "It's hard because of coronavirus these days, isn't it? How are you dealing with it now that you've lost all your customers?"

Then he told me, "It must be harder on you than me. I cannot imagine how hard it must be for you to provide paychecks for over twenty employees. I feel for you."

His words of comfort made me choke up. He was a fashion designer whom I had always admired, and he owned an off-line fashion shop. I called him because I was concerned about him and his business, and I wanted to console him. But it was he who offered a word of comfort to console me instead. I could feel his deep consideration for me when he was telling me that the situation was harder on me than on him, even though I knew that his business had taken a hard hit. And that was the moment when I realized what a heartwarming comfort sympathy could be.

After that, I decided to follow his example. Even when somebody tells me just out of courtesy, "It's hard these days, isn't it?" I always tell them, "It must be harder on you. I cannot imagine how hard it must be for you."

Now that the entire society is going noncontact because of the virus and even human relationships have come to a stop, isolation and loneliness are the emotions we feel most. In order to survive by keeping our distance from others, aren't we slowly losing the human relationships that are so dear to us? Lately, I'm growing more and more concerned. It often breaks my heart to hear people spewing hurtful words of suspicion and criticism instead of words of sympathy and consideration.

Corona is a highly contagious virus, and anybody could get infected at any time. You can get infected by unconsciously holding a handrail in the subway or pressing a button in an elevator. There is a possibility of infection anywhere we stay–in offices, restaurants, or parks. None of us can ever be sure of not catching the virus.

Nevertheless, when you are confirmed to have the virus,

you become the target of blame because information about your job, residence, and the places you've been to become public knowledge. Companies add more pressure by telling employees that they will hold them responsible if anything happens because they could end up having to shut down their businesses. In fact, I've heard that there are companies that keep employees who have tested positive for the virus away from the company and even fire them. While suffering from a life-and-death illness, coronavirus patients feel enormous guilt and pressure and even have to be subjected to the accusing glares of the people around them.

Some confirmed patients have terrified people by sneaking out of self-isolation or quarantine facilities without permission. Of course, they deserve to be criticized. But there are far more people without symptoms who have spread the virus while minding their own business and being forced to keep working to make a living. It is our instinct for survival to fear the coronavirus and want to stay away from it, yet we must be able to see our own faces in the faces of the confirmed patients. We can protect human dignity and our precious communities only when we can sympathize with their pain and fear.

What we need now is to welcome back those who have been released from quarantine and give them warm words of comfort for the trouble they must have gone through. It could be that they fought a painful battle on our behalf because it could easily have been us. This kind of social empathy, consolation, and warm encouragement is the most important legacy that we can leave behind after the pandemic.

It is also the most important spiritual legacy that we can leave, not just for ourselves but for our next generation as well. The first thought that hit me when I heard that schools would reopen was a deep concern. Considering how adults were so distrustful and critical about confirmed patients, what would happen to the children? If there were confirmed cases among children, wouldn't they become targets of bullying from other kids? And if that happened, how deeply would their feelings be hurt, and what would it be like to live in pain for the rest of their lives? How would they feel if after having grown up in this situation, they are faced with similar situations years from now? Would they think, "I will be in big trouble if I am confirmed. I'll be ousted from society without question," or will they think, "This is a problem that we can overcome together"?

The coronavirus pandemic will be over someday. And we'll survive. I hope that when it happens, our children will think of consideration and trust, not distrust. I hope they will choose courage instead of hatred. To make this happen, we grown-ups must support and encourage one another. I hope that even in times of disasters such as coronavirus, we will be able to reach out, comfort one another, and say, "It must be harder on you than me." The survival of relationships and trust is just as important as the survival of our lives.

Mental immunity varies from person to person. Different people's resilience and ability to recover are not the same. In this time of coronavirus, those of us who are willing to reach out to hold the hands of others, even if they are slower or weaker than we are, are most humane–the ones with heart. And heart will save us as we go through this most difficult time. I cheer for all those out there who are strug-gling and working hard to make a living. I cheer for them with all my heart.

EPILOGUE

I, TOO, WISH TO GO BACK TO THE
PRE-CORONAVIRUS WORLD

One Sunday afternoon, after finishing this manuscript, I made a cup of iced coffee and read the whole thing, from the first page to the last. I felt a sense of unfulfillment, which happens every time I finish writing a manuscript. I told myself, "I wish I had just one more week to work on it."

But I also felt a sense of bitterness in my heart. I told myself, "I wish I had never had to write a book like this." Why did I feel this way after working so hard to write it? In fact, MK Kim's *Reboot* is a book that was never planned. It would not have been published if it hadn't been for coronavirus. I guess that explains why I felt bitter and even sorrowful.

To be honest with you, I miss the pre-coronavirus times every day, and I wish I could return to those days again. If I had a choice, I would go back to the pre-coronavirus world in a heartbeat. Sure, there is a hidden opportunity in a crisis, but can a crisis ever be better than a peaceful daily routine? What's more, the world is evolving so fast in the aftermath of coronavirus that we are forced to rack our brains like we've never done before just to keep pace with it. We need to know about digital transformation, artificial intelligence, and blockchain. Frankly, these concepts are difficult to understand, and they make our lives even more complicated. Had there not been coronavirus, we might have simply stayed the same until we retired. But now, there is no way to avoid them. We cannot last more than a year without learning about them. It's annoying because there are so many things that we have to learn now, and it is also a little unnerving because we are not sure if we can do it. When you feel that way, remember how far you've come and try to renew your determination by telling yourself, "That's how life goes, and there's no law that says I can't make it!"

Every once in a while, I am saddened when I think about what my daily life was pre-coronavirus. I don't know if there is anything more pleasing and joyous than meeting friends, chatting and eating with them, holding their hands, patting them on the back, and going on a trip with someone to get away from it all. Life is what happens when you meet people face-to-face and interact with them.

When I miss those days, I look at photos from a year ago in which I was speaking and jumping excitedly in front of an audience of 1,000 people. In the pictures, people are sitting shoulder to shoulder without social distancing, and there is a fever in the air as people clap their hands, cry, and laugh. And I am in the scene.

I only allow myself to visit those memories once in a while because it's still too depressing to think of them often. It was the work that I loved most and that I've been doing almost every day for the last thirty years, but now it feels like nothing more than memories encapsulated in photos.

Those who had no boundary between life and work will understand it. The feeling is comparable to that of having lost one of your arms or legs, and it is closer to the grief you would feel if you had lost your beloved child. The ache won't go away with a simple "sorry" or "look for the silver lining." It hurts.

I still remember clearly how I felt in February 2020. It was the day when I had no speaking schedule and the day when I realized that there would be no more speaking in the foreseeable future. I felt as though I had been dropped in a strange place, even though I came to the same office as usual, and the same employees as usual were there. I had instantaneously landed in a different world, as if I were being pushed away.

I felt helpless and sad and the sense of loss. Having the thing I loved most taken away from me in an instant was devastating and filled me with deep sorrow. Those feelings were followed by numerous other emotions, which broke me down. I felt like a pathetic human who could not take responsibility for the company, and I felt as though I were suffocating, as day after day I watched money hemorrhaging from our accounts.

I'm sure that at this moment, many others share the same feelings. We have all left something that was dear to us in the pre-coronavirus world. Each of us has lost something precious: the cherished routines in which we laughed and chatted with friends at school or work; coworkers we cared about; the companies, shops, and customers who provided us with a living and made up our "field of dreams," and in my case, the time I had with my audience when I was on stage. We have an excruciating sense of loss. Many times while experiencing these emotions, I wanted to return to the old days. I didn't want to accept this reality.

But the moment I knew that the post-coronavirus world was quickly settling down and forging a new order, I had no time to hold on to the sense of loss. I had many things to do in order to keep and protect my family and my company.

We all feel the sense of loss to different degrees, and we have all lost different things, but there is one thing that we haven't lost: ourselves. We may have lost everything but not ourselves. For example, the thirty years in which the motivational speaker MK Kim made speeches on stage is gone, but MK Kim, the person, is not. I still try to carry out daily routines as I always did, dream little dreams, and be a decent person even in the new world.

The times that we loved are gone, but we are still here. It is just the world around us that has changed; we remain unchanged. And the workplace that I must keep and protect is still there, too. My only wish is to be a good person to the people I care about.

People say that as you get older, you worry more, and I couldn't agree more. As I got to know more about the post-coronavirus world while writing this book, I became so worried about so many people. When I met schoolteachers, I worried about them because they were supposed to learn and get themselves used to edu-tech, and when I met a younger friend of mine who is in the film industry, I worried about her because theaters might not be able to keep their doors open. Recently, I went to an alumni reunion, and whenever I had a chance to talk with my old school buddies, I preached to them about how they must adjust themselves to the digital world.

I wrote this book thinking of all the people that I worry about. I wrote wishing that you will not retreat or give up hope in the face of rapid changes, no matter what you do and what you dream. Instead, I hope you will start your dreams and your life all over again. I also thought of my children and the young people who will be living in the future world. I wanted to show what we have right before our eyes to the students and young adults who will live in the future, while learning more dynamically than at any other time. Because in this new world where there are no solid role models that have made their appearance yet, they will have to be their own role models.

Now is the time to rise. We must muster our courage and begin anew from where we stopped. We must move on from the sense of loss and fear. Our dreams and lives must go your own reboot.

Recently, I posted a short message on my Instagram.

"Hard, isn't it? But we are not alone. We can make it. Don't worry."

But I ended choking up while reading comments people made to that post. I guess they were all feeling withdrawn with an unexplainable sense of loss and anxiety. I'd never imagined my word, "don't worry," would garner so many comments.

Before closing this epilogue, I want to tell you this, too.

"We'll make it. So don't worry."